THE PRIORITY OF KNOWING GOD

THE
PRIORITY
OF KNOWING
GOD

Taking Time with God
When There Is No Time

REVISED EDITION

PETER V. DEISON

kregel
PUBLICATIONS

Grand Rapids, MI 49501

The Priority of Knowing God: Taking Time with God When There Is No Time

© 1990, 2000 by Peter V. Deison
Second Edition

Published by Kregel Publications, a division of Kregel, Inc., P.O. Box 2607, Grand Rapids, MI 49501. Kregel Publications provides trusted, biblical publications for Christian growth and service. Your comments and suggestions are valued.

For more information about Kregel Publications, visit our web page: http://www.kregel.com

Library of Congress Cataloging-in-Publication Data
Deison, Peter V.
  The priority of knowing God: taking time with God when there is no time / by Peter V. Deison.
      p.   cm.
  Includes bibliographical references.
  1. God—Worship and love. 2. Spiritual life. 3. Christian life. I. Title.
BV4817.D45   1990   248.4—dc20   90-33895
                                                                          CIP
ISBN 0-8254-2491-7

Printed in the United States of America

1 2 3 4 5 / 04 03 02 01 00

To my wife, Harriet,
a woman of excellence. She shines as the
brightest light among the motivators
behind this effort. Her consistent example
made the difference as we struggled
to learn what it means to meet with God.
Thank you, honey!

Contents

Part 3 • A Quiet Time "How-To"

Foreword

Do you ever find yourself putting your quiet time with God in the same category as dieting, jogging, and flossing your teeth—merely another good habit to be learned? Is your quiet time like liver and onions—something they say is good for you, but the benefits must be accepted by faith? Or perhaps you deeply understand the benefits and have developed a daily practice but seem to have lost the enjoyment and spontaneity that you saw in earlier times?

This book is not another shrill "do this because it's good for you" plea. In a fresh and long-overdue way, Pete Deison explains how your quiet time can become an intimate discussion with your best friend. He explains how we can enter into the quiet time with the anticipation of a long-awaited fishing trip rather than a long-dreaded trip to the dentist. As a result, what once was dry, routine, or even nonexistent in your life can become spontaneous and refreshing.

I have known Pete for almost two decades as a student, as a friend, and now as a colleague. He is a faithful man with a deep desire to help people develop in their thirst for God. This book is the result of years of thought, practice, defeat, and victory in the pursuit of a strong relationship with God.

The quiet time is somewhat of a mystery to most of us. If you are in the ranks of millions of Christians who have been told that you're always supposed to do it but never understood what it was and never really knew what would happen if it was done right, you will enjoy the insights Pete has for us all.

—HOWARD G. HENDRICKS

Preface

WE COME TO GOD ONLY because He has made Himself known to us. The all-powerful Creator has opened the door of mystery because He wants us to come. We would not know He existed if He didn't want us to know. We would not have a way to come if He did not provide a way. We would not know what He is like if He had not shown us Himself.

Because He has opened the way to know Him, and shown us that He can be trusted, He bids us to meet with Him. That call to come begins an amazing relationship. There is no other word for it but amazing. The discoveries astound us, confound us, and resound in our hearts, minds, and souls forever.

They astound us because as soon as we respond to His call, we are overwhelmed with majesty, power, purity, holiness, righteousness, and justice. Our immediate reaction is to pull away in fear and shame. Fear, because in the greatness and power we feel small. Shame, because the purity and holiness cause us to see our impurity and unholiness.

However, we are also confounded! Behind our fear and shame is a compelling warmth and growing desire to humbly come forward. We begin to recognize the experience of grace whether we understand it or not. We do not know enough to grasp that even the inner desire to come is His work.

Finally, there is a resounding joy that floods our heart, mind, and soul because we slowly understand that this majestic power, God Himself, has set His love upon us and made us holy, righteous and pure by satisfying His own demand for justice. He has freed us from the shame of our impurity and true guilt of our unholiness. He has removed the fear and given us boldness and confidence to come to His throne of majesty and seat of grace. Our hearts are compelled, our minds are rewarded, and our souls begin to resound with worship.

Acknowledgments

I would like to say thanks to:

Helen Deison (my mother)—who prayed before I was born that I would meet the Lord. She laid my foundation by her prayers and example.

Frank Kifer—who shared Christ with a young college student and stuck with me till I could stand on my own.

Bill Bright—who taught me what spontaneous time with God was like.

Howard Hendricks—who motivated my socks off, and challenged me never to settle for a mediocre time with God.

Ben Haden—who encouraged me to keep it practical.

Pat Hartman Page, Catherine Hellmann, Betsy Varner, Janice Anne McGhee, Rose Franks—who labored in love an untold number of hours typing this book.

Karen D'Arezzo—who did a superb editing job.

Introduction

AFTER TWENTY YEARS OF trying, failing, stumbling, and walking with Christ since writing the first draft of *The Priority of Knowing God*, I asked myself, "What have I learned? Have I changed my mind? What could I add?"

This book has given me many opportunities to speak to church groups, men's retreats, and seminary classes. I find the same thing over and over: People are hungry to meet with God. They ask essentially the same questions wherever I go. They want to know if they are doing it right and how their time with God can be better. I have learned that some things never change.

In revisiting this friend (I refer to it often myself), there is little I would change. I rewrote it three times over a ten-year period before it was published. I have not changed my mind on its solid points, but I have expanded my appreciation and understanding of them.

There is still a tremendous amount of guilt that either drives believers to a works sanctification (devotional life) or takes the simple joy and rest out of the relationship. We must conquer this enemy, which is not difficult to do once you understand the grace involved. The heartbeat of the book is found in the first three chapters. I only wish I could say it better so that the reader would never want those chapters to end. This is what it is all about.

In the rest of the book I focus on prayer, God's Word, and the process of getting involved in prayer and the Word of God. This automatically raises problems and questions—problems because we are sinners and questions because we are seekers.

Finally, there are many new resources, so I have added more helps in the bibliography. These will give you great satisfaction for years to come.

Again, what have these ensuing years taught me as I have met with God? The following thoughts and experiences have consumed many hours of my devotional life, some with joy, most with struggle, and all with awe at how faithful God has been.

- Life is full of pain even when you are right with God. Pain and prayer are partners.
- Some prayers take a long time because they are more valuable to God.
- As life has its cycles, so do our emotions and our spiritual growth. Dark nights of the soul are real and of great value.
- Too much of my prayer life is self-centered and not God-centered.
- There is a common reoccurring heresy of men who want to be stricter than God, and I fall prey so easily.
- Giving away your devotional treasures increases your treasury.
- It is so easy to drift afar if you don't pay careful attention, so prayer must be carefully protected.
- Prayer is first a response—only later can it become a request.
- Much of our prayer life is to achieve goals and to pray for others, yet little is done just to enjoy Him.
- Hebrews 2:1—You can drift away if you don't pay careful attention.
- Isaiah 57:15—God lives with those who are lowly in spirit.
- 1 John 3:20—We can set our hearts at rest in His presence.

PART ONE

Starting Right

CHAPTER ONE

Getting Past Guilt

Many people think God punishes our failures by giving us a second-class rating. No, failure should not produce depression, rather dependence. We do not serve Him to gain His favor. We serve Him because He has favored us.

—Unknown

THE REPORT CAME OVER the Associated Press wire service—a true confession to the IRS.

He wrote,"I have not been able to sleep well for two years. Here is my check for $1,200 for back taxes." He even signed his name, then added a short P.S. "If I don't sleep better in a week, I will send you another $1,200."

You can feel it. He had to do something to relieve his guilt, but he didn't want to do too much.

Sir Arthur Conan Doyle, author of the Sherlock Holmes mysteries, used to tell how he sent a telegram to each of twelve friends, all men of great virtue and reputation. The message read, simply, "Fly at once; all is discovered." Within twenty-four hours, the story goes, all twelve had left the country.

Guilt hangs on every one of us. Not the guilt of flagrant sin— we know how to deal with that. Obvious sin is too painful to hide when we know there is forgiveness. However, the guilt that hangs on in the back of our minds is the guilt of wondering if we have done enough for God, if we have given Him the time we should.

How many times have you felt like this? "My life goes so fast I just don't have the time for the Lord that I would like to have. I feel so bad about it, but I just don't know what to do. I don't know how many times I've tried to have a daily time with the Lord but it just doesn't seem to work. To be honest, I don't often get much out of my Bible, and yet sometimes it is really great. I wish it could be great all the time. It should be, I think. I must be missing something or it wouldn't be so hard. What can I do about it? I just feel so guilty."

Nothing kills the joy of meeting with God more thoroughly than guilt—yet it is so common. Recurring guilt is perhaps the most frequent struggle in our Christian lives. We wonder why we do not feel right with God or why we haven't spent more time with Him or for Him. Whether we call it quiet time, devotions, Bible study, or meditation, we feel guilty for not doing it long enough or well enough. Why isn't it better, deeper, easier, more enjoyable?

For most of us it is either miserable or missing or mysterious. Few Christians keep a growing edge in their meetings with God. Why? Why does the mention of a quiet time cause most of us to feel guilty—even for those who try? And most of us have tried, but we have puzzled over what it really should be, and we have felt miserable over our failures.

At a recent national seminar for Christian teachers and workers, a survey was taken of felt needs. The question was asked, What will you be the most ashamed of when you get to heaven and what will you wish you would have changed? The overwhelming response was *My personal devotional life*.

Why is this part of our faith so troublesome and so hard to grasp? The answer is found in knowing what we are pursuing.

I discovered in my response to God's call that there is supposed to be a growing awareness of my sin. God in His grace does not overwhelm me with all of my sin when I first began my journey toward Him. If He had, I could have never taken a closer step. He simply exposed my life enough with His light that I knew I could not come closer without Him. I did not know what I was pursuing, but something, or someone, was urging me on.

―――― *Reflection* ――――――――――――――――――

1. Would "guilty" accurately describe the way you feel about your devotional life?
2. Are your feelings of guilt based on the reality or the perception of your experience with God?
3. What would you most like to change about your meetings with God? Deeper insights? Better life applications?
4. What are you willing to do to achieve a more satisfying devotional life?

CHAPTER TWO

Pursuing the Personal

Secularism marginalizes and eventually obliterates the two essentials of human fullness: intimacy and transcendence. Intimacy: we want to experience human love and trust and joy. Transcendence: we want to experience divine love and trust and joy.
—Eugene Peterson, *Subversive Spirituality*

MORRIS DAVIS WAS PUT in jail for "praying." It all began when Davis was picked up and charged with arson. After his arrest, he was taken to a room at the police station for a lie detector test. Thinking he was alone, he prayed that old familiar prayer, "Lord, let me get away with it just this once." But a policeman overheard his prayer and submitted it as evidence against him.

The lower court ruled that this was a private conversation and therefore could not be submitted as evidence. The Canadian government, however, appealed this ruling and the Court of Appeals decided that it was admissible evidence because a prayer is not a private conversation, since God is not a person. Following this trial, an American newspaper picked up the story and ran it under the headline, "God Ruled a Non-Person."

Surprising? Not really. Men have always lived as if God were not a person. Most suspect that He exists but never live as if they expect to meet Him face to face—person to person.

Perhaps we make the same mistake. We claim a personal faith, yet our relationship to God is impersonal. We believe God is holy, righteous, almighty. But these qualities keep us from seeing Him as a person; they don't describe anyone we know. God then becomes someone we put on a pedestal so far above us that He ceases to be a real person.

The first answer to why we meet with God is to know Him as personally as possible.

This is the mystery of meeting with God. He is holy, righteous, and almighty, but He is a person first. He has made us relational beings, so we can know each other person to person. There is a sameness between God and us.

Looking at our origins gives us a clearer picture of this personal God. The first words of God concerning us were, "Let us make man in our image." It was not a flesh and blood image, but a person's image—a person who thinks, feels, loves, wills, desires, and even hurts.

He not only made us like Himself, but He actually became one of us so that we could know Him even better and could understand that we are like Him and that He is like us. This is another way of saying God sets His interests and desires upon us. He delights in us because He made us in His image.

Looking Like God

How does being made like God explain why we have devotions? Take a close look at that image again. It is an image of personality. And it includes intellect, emotions, and will.

God provided Adam with three experiences that helped him to understand how he was made in that image. The first was the experience of naming all the animals. Imagine the fun Adam had naming the big fat animal a hippopotamus or the skinny, long-necked one a giraffe—that must have been great! Using his own intellectual ability, Adam must have been awed by the vast, superior intellect of God. He was learning about the mind of God. Adam found that his mind was so made that he could know God. Their relationship involved two thinking persons.

Adam understood that he could think as God wanted him to think. So he brought his thoughts into line with the thoughts of God. God wants all of us to think as He thinks, because His thoughts are truth. And the truth is crucial for one person to know another.

The second experience God provided for Adam was marriage. God gave Adam a wife to meet the need for human companionship. In this experience, Adam learned to use his emotions by loving someone else. God wanted Adam to understand that he was a person with emotions. And believe me, it didn't take long after Eve entered the scene for Adam to understand that. Adam was thrilled that she was like him and not like a hippopotamus. But God not only wanted Adam to experience the emotions of loving and being loved, He wanted Adam to realize that *He* was a loving person. He showed His love for Adam by giving him Eve. So by being like God, Adam understood that God is loving, and he also learned that love is essential for us to know one another.

The third experience God gave Adam came in the form of a command—His personal request that he and his wife not eat the fruit of the tree of the knowledge of good and evil. In time Adam failed to follow through, but not before he learned about the will of God. He learned that God was a person of will and that he, too, was created in that image. He was given a will so that he might have the capacity to obey God. To have a personal relationship with God, he needed to know and respect God's will. So the freedom to choose is also vital to establish the respect two persons need to know each other.

God wanted Adam to see how much alike they were. He said in short, "Adam, I give you a *mind* to know Me and to bring into harmony with My mind; a *heart* to love Me and to bring into harmony with My heart; and a *will* to obey Me and to bring into harmony with My will."

God gave Adam what was in Himself so that Adam could fully enjoy a person-to-person relationship with Him. He was like God and could therefore know God to the fullest of his created ability.

Commenting on the experiences of Adam in *Designed To Be Like Him*, Dr. Dwight Pentecost said that what a man truly knows, he will love, and what he truly loves, he will serve. This is what being personal with God is all about—knowing, loving, and serving Him as Father. This is what makes a quiet time possible. God has made us so we can respond to Him and communicate with Him.

Why Is It So Hard to Be Personal?

The perfect image was corrupted. Because of Adam's disobedience and resulting sin nature, his opportunity to walk with God in the cool of the day was changed. Now our whole nature is changed. Our ability to know God has been darkened; our ability to love God has been degraded; and our ability to obey God has been disabled. We no longer naturally seek to know Him. We find it hard to love Him with pure motives. And it is with difficulty that we obey Him. It is no wonder God doesn't seem very personal.

This is what makes our personal friendship with God through Christ so special. Our old nature, or sin nature, no longer has to control us. We now have a new ability to get close to God (2 Corinthians 5:17–18). God wants to restore us to personal intimacy.

Paul tells us that God is changing our corrupted image into something better than, but like, the original image (2 Corinthians 3:18). We are being renewed and conformed into that image of God. The old nature is still with us, and we struggle with it as Paul relates in Romans 7 and Galatians 5. But God has given us a new capacity as Christians to know, to love, and to serve Him. Why? So we can actually see Him as He is—as we were meant to.

We can never get too personal with God because that is just what He desires. We have a quiet time to get personal with God—to know Him.

The Importance of Intimacy

This is what life is really about—to know God as deeply as we can. He created us like Himself so that we might know what He is like and know what He wants. Paul echoed this when he said that his life's goal was to know God through Jesus (Philippians 3:8). This is what God desires from us. He wants our priority to be knowing and enjoying Him as Lord and friend.

J. I. Packer, author of the modern-day masterpiece *Knowing God*, says:

> What were we made for? To know God. What aim should we set ourselves in life? To know God. What is the "eternal life" that Jesus gives? Knowledge of God. "This is life eternal, that they might know thee, the only true God, and Jesus Christ, whom thou hast sent" (John 17:3). What is the best thing in life, bringing more joy, delight, and contentment, than anything else? Knowledge of God. "Thus saith the Lord, 'Let not the wise man glory in his wisdom, and let not the mighty man glory in his might, nor let the rich man glory in his riches; but let him that glorieth glory in this, that he understandeth and knoweth me' " (Jeremiah 9:23 ff.). What, of all the states God ever sees man in, gives Him the most pleasure? Knowledge of Himself. "I desire . . . the knowledge of God more than burnt offerings," says God (Hosea 6:6).

Getting personal with God begins with knowing. The more deeply we know the more fully we can love, and the more fully we love the more completely we can serve.

The key to unraveling the quiet time question is realizing that it is not a thing, or a feeling, but a relationship. It begins with one person's desire to be with another. Actually, *quiet time* does not tell the whole story—*devotions* comes closer to capturing the idea. It is a time devoted to a person. So the first answer to why we meet with God is to know Him—personally.

And it gets even better. Not only can we know Him person-ally, we can be counted as His friends.

—— *Reflection* ————————————————

1. Since you are made in God's image, how does that affect the way you relate to Him?
2. Who is your closest friend? What makes your relation-ship with him or her special?
3. Why must knowledge of God come before intimacy with God? How does that affect the way you approach your time of devotion to Him?
4. What part does service have in your devotional life?

CHAPTER THREE

Finding Friendship

Friendships multiply joys and divide griefs.
—H. G. Bohn

A friend is someone who can see through you and still enjoy the show.
—*Farmers Almanac*

I FEEL JEALOUS WHEN I read how God called Abraham and Moses His friends. What a privilege!

We talk about a personal relationship with God, but if we're honest, it isn't very personal. Our relationship with Him may be like many other relationships, good but not intimate. Personal relationships are the ones that bring deep satisfaction and significance to our lives.

Not long ago I was thinking about friendship with God. I enjoyed my relationship with Him, but when I was alone with Him, I did not feel like "a friend of God." I knew that it should be the closest of all my relationships. But in honesty it was not. I felt much closer to my wife and to my best friends than I did to God. I was not halfhearted. I was sincere. I often saw His unique work in my life—some days more obviously than others. Yet, even though I knew He was always present, I did not have the closeness that I desired. I asked myself, "If I really love God

28

and all that He has done for me, why don't I sense a more personal closeness with Him?" While searching for an answer to that question, I discovered two major barriers to friendship with God.

The Barrier of Formality

Most of us have been taught to revere God. We learn to pray using King James English. Seventeenth-century English is beautiful, no doubt, but it can cause us to place God on a pedestal. "Thee" and "Thou" language tends to separate us from God. It can make us feel overly removed from Him. The King James Version was originally written for the common man, when "Thee" and "Thou" were the ordinary terms of the common man's language. So while the reverent tone of the King James language is beautiful and appropriate, especially in public worship, I am speaking now of our private time with God, where formality *can* interfere.

We are His children, and He is our Father. We are family. He has gone to great lengths to adopt us, that we might be close special family members. And He desires that kind of friendship with us.

We don't call our parents Mr. Watson or Mrs. White; rather, we call them by a term they give themselves, such as Mom or Dad.

Jesus did not have a barrier of language formality. But the Jews had lost the idea of an intimate personal God, and they were offended when Jesus called Himself God's Son and thus claimed that God was His Father. They understood the idea of God as Father, but did not understand why Jesus called Him "Abba"—Father. *Abba* was the name young children used, like daddy or papa. It was a warm word that showed unquestioning trust. In Romans 8:15, Paul affirms that we are adopted as God's children and can therefore call Him "Abba."

On a visit to Jerusalem, one day I found myself walking down a narrow valley between some apartments and shops. As I came around a corner I startled a small child. She immediately jumped up and ran to the door of her house saying, "Abbi, Abbi," my daddy, my daddy. This is the call Jesus taught us; pray saying Abbi—My Father.

So, the very terms we use may reflect the degree of closeness we enjoy with God. Many cultures actually have language distinctions for closeness. The French, for instance, use different words for *you*, *we*, and *us* when speaking with someone who is not a family member or close personal friend. Could our formality in language be an unrealized barrier to closeness with God? It was for me.

The Barrier of the Impersonal

The barrier of an impersonal God is similar to the first but goes a step further.

What makes us say, "Karen is the personal type" or "Jack is too impersonal"? What we mean is that one person is open, honest, and friendly, while the other is reserved and distant.

When we identify our closest friends, we usually point to those with whom we can be ourselves. With them we can share our unguarded opinions, our gut feelings, and our dreams without reservations, and they do the same with us. As we do, our friendships grow even deeper. This is what makes friendships personal.

But it must go two ways. When we seek a closeness with God we must remember this. God wants us to know Him deeply because He knows what knowing Him will do for us. But all too often we only come to God to get Him to do things for us without really seeking to know Him.

A *crucial error* in meeting with God *is thinking that the time spent is primarily for ourselves.* It isn't. It is first of all for Him. We so often come to Him with a "gimme gimme" attitude. We can easily begin to think that God must meet *our* needs and give *us* answers to *our* problems. He will and He does, but we do not treat Him as a real person when we take such a position. We wouldn't dare go to a friend or to our mate with request after request and nothing to give. And God is no different. We are devoting time to Him; our purpose is to give and not only to receive.

If we never give to God, He quickly becomes impersonal—even less, merely a source for answers or things. If He is a stranger to me, it is because I haven't devoted myself to knowing Him and giving of myself to Him. Giving is what regains the personal with God. Remember to keep in mind that God is continually being revealed to us. This is the work of the Holy Spirit, "He will take of Mine and declare it to you" (John 16:15b NKJV).

First Things First

Then what about our needs? It is not, of course, wrong to come to God with real needs. But we must first come to Him with an attitude of love and trust rather than an attitude that insists we be satisfied. He always bends His ear to our needs (Matthew 7:7–12), but how sad it is if all He hears is just another request (James 4:3). Solomon said in Ecclesiastes 5:1–2:

> Guard your steps as you go to the house of God, and *draw near to listen* rather than to offer the sacrifice of fools; for they do not know they are doing evil. Do not be hasty in word or impulsive in thought to bring up a matter in the presence of God. For God is in heaven and you are on the earth; therefore let your words be few. (NIV, italics mine)

How often we run into God's presence with our urgent requests with never a thought of the *person* He is or His desires!

Certainly there is a place for urgent needs and prayers. Nehemiah 2:4 shows us that. Nehemiah had no time to do anything but shoot the quick arrow of prayer into heaven, flaming with the need of urgent wisdom. And God graciously gave it.

The purpose of the devotional life, however, is first to present ourselves to God as loving, obedient servants. God has called us to be servants who desire to please Him. We are to be servants who know our Master as a loving, faithful master—one who is eager to meet our needs.

Jesus put it this way, "Seek first the kingdom of God and His righteousness, and all these things shall be added to you" (Matthew 6:33 NKJV). In other words, seek God and His interests; and God will meet your interests.

Once we get over the formality and impersonal barriers and begin to treat God as close and real, we will find a new freedom with Him. Remembering that God is a person with His own desires and interests will change our whole idea about spending time with Him. This is, in fact, the *most significant discovery* we will ever make about devoting time to Him.

Is God a non-person to you? Or is He reachable and special, as well as holy and sovereign? Recognizing His greatness and our sinfulness prompts our proper caution, but knowing Him as a person of grace and as one who has made us His own permits us to enter into deep personal friendship.

The psalmist puts it this way, "Friendship with God is reserved for those who reverence Him, with them alone He shares the secrets of His promises" (Psalm 25:14 LB). That puts it all together. Notice the respect in reverence and yet the deep personalness of the sharing of promises. It is give first—then receive friendship.

This is what God our Father has already done for us. He gives His Friendship to us, not because we deserve it; just the opposite. Even while we were enemies, Paul says, God revealed us to Himself. Jesus said to His disciples and to us, "I no longer call you servants, because a servant does not know his master's business. Instead, I have called you friends, for everything that I have learned from my Father I have made known to you." (John 15:15 NIV)

So a second answer to why we have a quiet time is to become God's friend. Yet there is even more!

—— *Reflection* ——————————————————

1. When you examine your devotional time, do you find that you often do it because you need something?
2. Is it possible to be too personal with God?
3. Are reverence for God and friendship with God incompatible?
4. How is a relationship with God similar to or different from a relationship with a spouse or a good friend? How does the quality of your devotional life contribute to your relationship with God?

CHAPTER FOUR

Learning to Love

Intimacy in marriage is simply the measure of the degree to which mutual self-disclosure is carried out.

—David Mace

DAVE MACON AND JOEL STRINGER were enjoying their long-awaited vacation in the Welsh mountains. On a warm day that July they met Kirk, a friendly shepherd boy, and asked him to join them for lunch. In time they found the discussion turning to Christ. As he asked questions, Kirk found the ultimate friendship he had been looking for. He trusted Christ as His Savior. As they left, they wanted to leave him with something to strengthen his understanding of Christ's love for him. They told him to re-member five words—one each for the thumb and fingers of his left hand—The Lord Is My Shepherd.

The following summer Dave and Joel went back to the same Welsh village, eager to find Kirk. Instead, their hearts ached as his mother told them that he had been killed from a fall the winter before. Kirk's mother told them they had been puzzled about his death, because when they found him he was grasping his third finger with his right hand. Dave and Joel remembered the saying they had taught Kirk. The third finger bears the symbol of possession—My. The young shepherd boy had died claiming possession by His Shepherd—the one who loved him and the one whom he loved.

Because the third finger represents possession, a gold ring is placed on that finger in marriage. The ancients believed that a nerve went directly from this finger to the heart—the center of affection. So, when a man and woman place a ring on each other's fingers, they are claiming possession of each other's love.

Married love does say something nothing else can say because of possession—the claim we can rightly make on each other's love. As much as marriage is ridiculed today, it is still sought after even by those who have failed over and over. Why? Because we all desire the depth of that type of love in our lives. This level of intimacy and commitment is what God wants to have with us.

The Marriage Model

Marriage has a high priority in God's plan. God gave it to meet an immediate need—companionship. Yet, as in everything God gives, it has deeper value. It was also given to demonstrate a higher spiritual truth. It is the best way to understand how deep friendship with God can be. In a very real sense God is saying, "I will marry you."

The Old Testament book of Hosea specifically uses marriage to describe God's desired relationship with us. In Hosea 2:19, God says to His people, "I will betroth you to Me forever" (NKJV). In the New Testament, Paul says in Ephesians 5 that we are the bride to Christ. In a very real sense God is saying, "Will you marry me?" He offers Himself—His love, His friendship. God is showing us that friendship with Him is like friendship in marriage—a friendship of love.

Love is a priority. Jesus explains the great commandment and its priority for us. He says, "The first [commandment] is, . . . 'Love the Lord your God with all your heart, and with all your soul, and with all your mind, and with all your strength' " (Mark 12:30 NKJV). He did not remind us of the greatest commandment because God must force us to love Him. He reminded us with His words and life so we would understand that God wants to have a love relationship with us.

A natural question then follows, and it is one that I ask my- self: If marriage is an example of God's relationship to me, what makes my love friendship with my wife Harriet so differ- ent from my relationship with Him? Why do Harriet and I have a love for each other that we do not share with anyone else? Would understanding this love help me in my friendship with God? This idea made me look back to the beginning of my love friendship with Harriet, especially our engagement.

It is such a refreshing time to remember. I'll never forget the day after we got engaged. I was walking to class, thinking only of Harriet. As I climbed the stairs that led into the building, with my head in the clouds, I didn't quite make the top step. I tripped, fell, tore my pants, and cut my knee. Without realizing where I was, I rolled over. Because I was on a sharp incline, however, I rolled down into the street. Lying in the gutter, cov- ered with mud and leaves, I still could think only of Harriet.

As the water seeped through the back of my shirt, I sud- denly realized what had happened and jumped up. The bell was ringing and, without thinking, I ran into the classroom. Because the door was at the front of the class, everyone looked, and there I stood—torn pants' leg, blood, mud, and leaves. I didn't know what to say. All I could think of was, "I'm in love." After an embarrassing explanation to friends, everyone under- stood and no further questions were asked. Love often explains our circumstances and actions, especially when we become to- tally absorbed in another person.

Thinking then of my marriage, I saw it as a two-way love friendship with an ultimate aim. The aim is to become totally united with that special person. A growing sense of oneness is what produces more and more enjoyment, satisfaction, and ful- fillment. And if that is true with our husband or wife, then it must be true with God. But how do we achieve that oneness?

There are definite steps that enable us to find this personal closeness with God—the same ones that build a marriage. Three are basic to a healthy relationship:

1. First and foremost, marriage is a commitment.

Following our engagement day, Harriet began to experience some doubts about this permanent step. However, based on what I knew about Harriet, the circumstances of my own life, and answered prayers, God had confirmed in my mind that Harriet was the one for me. So I told her, "I'll wait as long as I have to, because I already know that you are the one God has for me." Later she told me that my confidence gave her confidence about our future marriage.

Isn't it the same with God? He has committed Himself to us. He has made an agreement for us without even getting our okay. He has said He would never leave us or forsake us. He calls it a covenant. It is a promise He will not break.

The word in the Old Testament that best expresses this idea is the Hebrew word *hesed*. It is translated "lovingkindness" in most Bibles (Psalms 100:5; 106:1; 136). Yet a clearer translation is "loving loyalty." God has a loyal love for us—unwavering, unconditional, unending loyalty.

This idea of commitment or loyalty is clearly seen in the Roman soldier that was uncovered in the ruins of Pompeii. His skeleton, encased in full armor and clutching a spear and shield with bony fingers, was found at its post in the ruined city. His skeleton was found alone. All other inhabitants of that great city, the officials, merchants, priests, and scholars, had fled to safety as Mount Vesuvius erupted. Alone, this sentry had stood fast as the lava covered the city. Loyalty prompted him to stay at his post while the world shook around him—to remain even to death.

This is God's commitment to us. This kind of commitment is the quality of love that makes it easier for us to commit ourselves to Him.

Just as commitment in marriage is vital, so it is in our friendship with God. Commitment to friendship with God gives security.

Yet, when we know that God's commitment to us never wavers, even when ours does, we still have security. My grip on Him may fail, but His grip on me never does. It is this security that we need when crises come and suddenly make God appear distant.

2. A healthy marriage must have communication.

Marriages grow in direct proportion to the amount of healthy communication.

I'll never forget the shock I received after five years of what I thought was a good marriage. I discovered that my wife and I were not really communicating. There were many disappointments, frustrations, and desires that we had buried. We were not facing the responsibilities of communicating about some of the painful areas in our marriage. We had not taken the time to explain our motives and desires. We had just hoped the other would get the hint. I guess we each expected the other to be a mind reader.

Likewise, how many times do we fail to communicate our real desires and feelings to God? Is God getting the short end of our communication? Are we really honest with Him? Do we work at listening to Him through His Word to understand His desires and commands? This is what healthy communication is all about. We speak to Him in prayer, and He speaks to us in His Word.

God says He can speak to us from any place in the Bible (2 Timothy 3:16). He communicates to us when He uses our own thoughts and informs us through our minds as we consider what He says in His Word.

I used to wonder why God didn't speak out loud anymore or do any more Red Sea style miracles. It finally dawned on me that everything God wants to say has already been said in His Word, miraculously preserved for us. God's Spirit makes His Word on the page come alive in our minds, so that we might think His thoughts each time we read them. This is God's communication to us. We don't need to look for the unusual, like voices and visions. God can do the unusual, but that is the exception. His communication to us is complete in the Bible. Seek His thoughts there and you will never be disappointed or confused about any other spiritual experiences you may have. True spiritual experiences never contradict the clear message of God in Scripture.

Good communication in marriage, then, is found when two people are committed to speaking of their deep desires and real needs with one another and to asking enough questions to know that they have heard and understood the other clearly. God doesn't have any needs, of course, but He does desire to have that same kind of companionship with us. He desires to enjoy our love and to hear our prayers. He is a great listener and is even called the Wonderful Counselor. He also loves for us to listen to Him. Are we listening?

3. The most enjoyable element of a marriage friendship is communion.

Communion, which comes from the words *common* and *union*, is seen when two people are united in a common heart, mind, and strength—when two people begin to have much of life in common. It is seen in the experience of beginning to think each other's thoughts before they are expressed. Love is communicated, yet words may not be spoken. It is the simple enjoyment of being in one another's company.

Janie came into her house one day, sat down on a chair, and watched her mother iron clothes. After a moment her mother asked, "Janie, what do you want?" The little girl, without ever taking her eyes off her mother, said, "Nothing, mother. I just want to sit here, watching and loving you." It is the same in marriage.

When you are married, you enjoy those moments when your mate looks at you with love, approval, and acceptance. It feels good. You and God can enjoy the same communion. This comes when we ponder and think about Him, this wonderful person, God. It is when we worship Him for who He is—not just for some favorable thing He might do for us—that we are communing. And

God enjoys thinking about us, too. Psalm 139:17–18 tells us that God's thoughts toward us are more numerous than we can count.

These three elements—commitment, communication, and communion—bring the sense of completion to marriage.

In the same way marriage is a life devoted to the needs and desires of another first, your quiet time is primarily to show devotion to God. Paul said that if you love your wife like Christ loved the church, you will really be loving yourself. Seeking to meet her needs first will motivate her to meet your needs. A sense of completion and security naturally follows.

Theodore Bovet put it this way in *Handbook for Marriage*: "I have bound myself for life; I have made my choice: from now on my aim will not be to choose a woman who will please me, but to please the woman I have chosen."

Our meeting with God is the time we first give to the One we love and then let Him give to us. He has already committed Himself to love us and meet our needs.

In *Knowing God*, J. I. Packer quotes James Orr, who said:

"Love, generally, is that principle which leads one mortal being to desire and delight in another, and reaches its highest form in that personal fellowship in which each lives in the life of the other, and finds his joy in imparting himself to the other, and in receiving back the outflow of that other's affection unto himself. Such is the love of God. . . ." This is all the more significant when we remember God was happy without man before man was made; He would have continued happy had He simply destroyed man after man had sinned, but as it is He has set His love upon particular sinners, and this means that, by His own, free, voluntary choice, He will not know perfect and unmixed happiness again till He has brought every one of them to heaven. *He has in effect resolved that henceforth for all eternity His happiness shall be conditioned upon ours* (italics mine).

God has so wedded Himself to us that even His own happiness depends upon ours.

Are we committed to God in a love friendship like that? Are we communicating our deepest thoughts and desires to Him and listening to Him through His Word? Are we enjoying communion and expressing love to Him? If not, these vital parts of the love friendship can begin today. We are never more than a prayer away from fresh commitment, open communication, and fulfilling communion with God. It begins with desire and confession. This is how we get personal with God.

Remember, God will never love us more than He loves us right now. No matter who we are or what we've done. God has committed Himself to love us, and it is His desire that we open our lives to an intimate friendship with Him. If we don't, we miss the real person.

So a third step to having a quiet time is to give and receive love as we enjoy this deepest part of friendship with God.

Now friendship with God, like marriage, sounds good, but how do we practically live it out?

------ *Reflection* ------------------------------

1. What parts do commitment, communication, and communion play in your experience with God?
2. How can you apply the principles of a good marriage—or any other close friendship—to your relationship with God?
3. How can God enjoy us?
4. What difference does it make to you that, to some extent, God's own happiness is conditioned upon your own?

CHAPTER FIVE

Wanting Worship

The end we ought to purpose to ourselves is to become in this life, the most perfect worshippers of God we can possibly be.

—Brother Lawrence,
Practicing the Presence of God

THEY WERE ANGRY. It looked as if fourteen years of marriage were about to end. "You have never loved me and you never will," she told him. In exasperation, he said, "It isn't true; I do love you. I have done everything I can for you. I've worked hard to provide you with a home and a car, and I've given you and the kids everything you need. Would I have done all this if I didn't care about you?"

"But you won't even talk to me," she said. "I don't really know you. You are only interested in your job."

Here are two people who cared for one another, but did not know how to express their love. She didn't see his love for her shown in hard work and provision. He didn't see her love for him expressed in her desire to be part of his life. Neither felt loved. Each felt so strongly about his or her personal needs that neither could see the other's affection.

Saying I Love You

This mysterious problem of failing to understand another person's love is masterfully explained in Judson Swihart's compact book entitled *How Do You Say, "I Love You?"* We have all tried to love someone and experienced frustration when we learned that the other didn't think we cared. Swihart illustrates from his years of family counseling that different people express love differently. Each of us learns certain ways to express love. When we marry or form a close friendship, we naturally begin to express our love toward that person. Yet, we find that it may not be accepted or appreciated and our feelings are hurt.

Swihart compares that situation to a German boy falling in love with a Chinese girl. They both love each other but do not speak each other's language. In time, problems develop, because no matter how desperately she tells him in Chinese she loves him, he will understand very little. She, in turn, will feel unloved because no matter how hard he tries to say he loves her, she will not be able to understand or appreciate his German.

We are like that with each other. We have learned different languages of love during our childhood and often do not recognize when someone eagerly expresses love through certain actions. We must learn each other's language of love. We only truly love another person when we love him the way he wants to be loved—the way he understands love.

If we only feel loved when others love us in a way we understand, is it possible God also wants us to love Him in a certain way? If we have feelings of love and gratitude toward God, how can they best be expressed?

A Personal Discovery

I can remember being dissatisfied with my devotional life as a young Christian. It had become so distasteful that I began to skip it. Then I heard some older Christians say that they often prayed for an hour or more. Wow! I thought . . . more dedication to prayer—that had to be the solution.

I will never forget the afternoon I set out to pray as long as I could. The whole afternoon was before me. The clock was on my desk and I began to pray. I prayed and prayed about everything I could think of. It seemed like forever. When I finally opened my eyes and looked at the clock, seven minutes had gone by. What a disappointment! I continued to wrestle with a miserable devotional time.

At this time I was working with Campus Crusade for Christ in Tennessee. One night several of us drove to Chattanooga to pick up Bill Bright, president of Campus Crusade. On our way back to Knoxville he said, "Let's pray as we drive back." I learned something that night that changed my time with God.

Before long it was evident that Bill's prayers were different. It was as if the rest of us weren't even in the car. He was praying as if the greatest person in the whole world was right there with us. And He was.

That's what I had never done—treated God as the greatest person in the world.

Bill began to tell the Lord how much he loved and worshiped Him. It was not a big emotional high, but simply a man pouring out his heart to a person he loved.

I began to ask myself why I couldn't pray that way. Have you ever felt like that? Somebody prays and you think, "I wish I could pray like that." The enjoyment of that prayer, though, is not in the words. It is in the understanding and heart of the person who prayed. Still struggling, I kept at it.

One day, not long after that, I was reading in the Psalms and came across some of the phrases Bill had used. He had been putting verses from the Psalms into his own words as he prayed. I decided to give this a try. At first it was awkward, but in a short time the words became my own. I began to express my love, praise, and worship to God in a new way, using the verse words He had provided in Scripture. My personal consciousness of the Lord as a person began to grow. Seeing Him as a real person and loving Him as a real person became downright exciting. It was like a boy finding out for the first time that girls really are neat. I discovered genuine pleasure in quiet time.

Eugene Peterson has written the best treatment of Psalms as tutors of prayer. His book, *Answering God,* explains that the Psalms were written for the purpose of teaching us how to respond to our heavenly Father. God has spoken first and all prayer is simply answering Him. I had stumbled onto this most valuable truth and it enabled me to take the most significant step I would take in understanding time with God, the step of worship.

I didn't realize it then, but this is what worship is actually all about—the expression of pleasure in words of praise and respect. As I continued to read the Bible, it began to dawn on me that worship was a major theme in the Scriptures. I decided to study to see what the Bible had to say about loving God through worship. When lovers say they worship each other, it is really the deepest way they know how to say they love one another.

Worship is God's language. That is what love means to Him. Let's look back into how God taught this to His people. It begins with Moses getting away to meet with God.

The Tent of Meeting

It was not a secret place and yet secrets were shared there—secrets of the deepest kind. The place was a tent away from all the other tents. Moses would go out to it every day and talk with God, and God would talk with him.

The Bible says, "The Lord used to speak to Moses face to face, just as a man speaks to his friend" (Exodus 33:11). We know Moses didn't see God's actual face, because God said no one can see His face and live; but Moses and God were friends, and they talked as if face to face. God's presence was there.

Moses named it the Tent of Meeting because it was there that he met with God. The name, Tent of Meeting, remained for almost 500 years until Solomon built the stone temple. For Israel it was always the place of the presence of God and His worship. It was there they dealt publicly and privately with their God.

Meeting with God and worshiping Him went together. In his book called *Worship*, A. W. Tozer said that worship is "an active effort to close the gap between the heart and the God it adores."

Today the residence of God is within the heart. Our worship is no longer focused on a building. We can now worship God without going to a tent or building. Private worship occurs when we bring our praise and honor as well as our deepest secrets, desires, needs, and hurts to a God who is waiting to meet with us face to face.

You might be saying, "I understand public worship, but what is private worship?" To understand it, let's look at the whole of worship.

This Is Worship

Worship literally means "worth-ship." It is ascribing worthiness to an individual. It means to pay reverence or to honor. The New Testament uses three different words for worship. The word used most often, *proskueno,* means to kiss the hand or to bend the knee. It is a recognition of the worth of the person. The other two words, *seromi* and *latrueo,* mean to fear and to serve, respectively. They refer to the attitude one should have (honor or reverence) and the action one should take (service) as a result of honoring that person. It is significant that the word for "godliness" in the New Testament means "good worship." Put these thoughts together and good worship involves recognizing worth, granting respect, and giving service.

The main Old Testament word means "to fall down in order to honor." It has an even stronger idea of the attitude one should have toward God and how this should affect us. I used to think of worship only as it related to Israel and something I was supposed to do in the church. Getting an overview of worship helped me realize that I should personally worship the Lord.

A Brief Survey of Worship in the Old Testament

From Genesis to Malachi, the matter of worship is found in

almost every book. The word *worship* is found 196 times in the Bible, and the word *praise* is found 277 times.

Beginning with Genesis, we find that Adam knew what it was to love and worship God. And Adam taught it to his children. In Genesis 4, Cain and Abel bring sacrifices to the Lord. The writer of Hebrews comments on Abel's offering, and it is no accident that the author records Abel's worship as the first act of faith on his list. Faith begins with worship. In Genesis 8, we find a grateful Noah building an altar to God to worship Him after the Flood. The new world began with worship.

Genesis 12 and following plunges us into the life of Abraham, that rugged patriarch. Everywhere he went, when he was in tune with God, he built an altar and worshiped (Genesis 12:7; 13:4, 18; 22:9). After two hundred years of bondage, God tells Moses to tell Pharaoh, "Let My people go," and not just so they can be free (Exodus 5:1, 8:1). He wants His people to go that they may come out and worship (Exodus 3:12). The last half of the book of Exodus is concerned solely with the building of the tabernacle so that Israel might worship and fellowship with God.

Leviticus is devoted to Israel's worship. It tells us how to approach God. Leviticus describes five offerings Israel had for worship.

1. The Burnt Offering was for dedication, setting oneself aside for the Lord.
2. The Meal Offering showed a recognition of God's goodness and provision for needs.
3. The Peace Offering was for restoring fellowship with God.
4. The Sin Offering was a recognition that we are sinners.
5. The Trespass Offering was for individual sin.

The period of the Judges is characterized by a lack of worship and a continual falling away from the Lord. The period of the Kings is the same. The kings were to be God's instruments to point the people to God. The ones whom the Bible considered successful were those who worshiped the Lord. David was made the standard by which all the kings were judged. David's great desire in life was to build a temple for the worship of God, a proper house in which God could dwell among His people. All the kings that follow David stand or fall on the basis of their faithful worship of God.

The largest section of the Bible is the Psalms. They were designed for the worship of God. They were the songbook for Israel's worship. Most of them are David's alone moments with God written that we might get a glimpse of this man's private worship. You will always find the Psalms express the feelings of your heart to the Lord.

The next period in the Bible is that of the prophets. They continually remind Israel to stay true to God and worship Him. Isaiah and Ezekiel, along with the book of Revelation in the New Testament, give us the greatest glimpses of heaven where worship is always found.

In the period of restoration, after Israel's captivity and return, one of its main tasks is to rebuild the temple. The last few books of the Old Testament, especially Zechariah and Malachi, blast Israel for its empty worship.

From beginning to end the Old Testament places a major emphasis on the worship of God.

A Brief Survey of Worship in the New Testament

The New Testament is no different. Matthew opens with the wise men coming to worship Jesus and closes with the disciples worshiping Jesus. In Matthew 4 we note an astounding fact about worship. The last and strongest temptation given to Jesus by Satan involves worship. Satan said he would give Jesus all the kingdoms of the world, "if You will fall down and worship me" (Matthew 4:9 NKJV). The thing the Devil wanted more than anything else was worship. He still does. So if that is what he wants, it must be the greatest thing we can give.

At the end of the Gospels, the church is launched with worship in the first chapters of Acts. During the period of history covered by Acts, Paul's writings give us numerous key passages.

In Romans 12:1, Paul uses the language and symbols of the temple, explaining that we are to be a living sacrifice. But notice the reason—it is our "spiritual service of worship." In other words, view your service as worship. In 1 Corinthians 3:16 Paul reminds us, "Do you not know that you are the temple of God and that the Spirit of God dwells in you?" (NKJV). We are no longer like the Israelites who had to go to a temple where God dwelt; rather God dwells in us. We are a temple. But think about it—what is a temple for? Worship. We are living, walking places of worship.

Peter builds on an Old Testament idea of worship in his first letter. He says we "are being built up as a spiritual house for a holy priesthood, to offer up spiritual sacrifices acceptable to God" (1 Peter 2:5). We are priests! We are to proclaim the greatness of God and let the world see our worship! What, then, did the priest do?

- Cared for the Temple
- Proclaimed the Lord's Word
- Interceded for others
- Offered sacrifices

Are we still to offer sacrifices today? Yes! Scripture describes at least five:

1. The sacrifice of praise (Hebrews 13:15; Psalm 50:23)
2. The sacrifice of repentance (Psalm 51:17; Isaiah 57:15)
3. The sacrifice of our body (Romans 12:1; Philippians 2:17)
4. The sacrifice of our work (Hebrews 13:16)
5. The sacrifice of our witness (Romans 15:15–16)

Finally, two of the most powerful passages on worship in the Bible are given to us by John in Revelation 4 and 5. To get a magnificent view of heavenly worship, take Revelation 4:11 and 5:12–13 and put them in your own words as praise to God. It will give you a great opportunity to express His language of praise to Him.

This abbreviated survey of the New Testament shows the same emphasis on worship as in the Old Testament.

As you followed this survey of worship you might have noticed the narrowing of the focus of worship from the nation of Israel in the Old Testament to the individual in the church in the New Testament. Jesus put this focus clearly before us.

God Seeks Only Our . . .

Jesus came to restore us to a right relationship with God, a loving friendship with Him. In John 4:21–24 He said something to the woman at the well that reached out and grabbed me forcefully. The woman had become uncomfortable and tried to sidetrack Jesus by discussing religion, yet He said:

> Woman, believe Me, an hour is coming when neither in this mountain, nor in Jerusalem, shall you worship the Father. You worship that which you do not know; we worship that which we know; for salvation is from the Jews. But an hour is coming, and now is, when the true worshipers shall worship the Father in spirit and truth; for such people the Father seeks to be His worshipers. God is spirit; and those who worship Him must worship in spirit and truth.

God is seeking people to be His worshipers, according to what Jesus said to the woman. There is *no other place in the Bible* where it says that God is seeking something from us. This is what God wants from us. And it's the only thing He wants from us because when He has true worship, He has all the rest. That is why Satan wanted Jesus' worship.

René Pache, in his book *The Person and Work of the Holy Spirit*, said, "The highest form of service is worship." Jesus Himself said, "Let your light shine before men in such a way that they may see your good works, and glorify your Father who is in heaven" (Matthew 5:16). In other words, true worship produces true service that is glorifying to God.

In *Unger's Bible Dictionary*, Dr. Merrill Unger says, "It is as natural to worship as it is to live—the feeling and expression of high adoration, reverence, trust, love, loyalty and dependence upon a higher power, human or divine, is a necessity to men. To these sentiments, to a greater or lesser degree, in every man, something or somebody, real or imaginary, appeals. And that something secures his worship." God has given us an inner desire to express worship. Man is free to give it to whomever he wishes. God is seeking it from us as a freewill expression of our faith and love.

Getting What He Came For

Several years ago, Tom Jackson was driving in Japan. As he drove along, he saw the little red oil light come on. He knew he needed to get somewhere quickly. He turned into the first service station he saw, and as he drove up, five Japanese men came running out the door.

In Japan service is a big thing. As Tom pulled in, one guy leaped over the car and began putting gas in the tank. Another checked all the tires for air. A third washed every window. A fourth raised the hood, checked the radiator and battery, and slammed the hood. The last fellow handed him a ticket. He paid and drove off. He went about two blocks when the little red oil light began to blink again.

The station attendants, it turned out, gave him everything except the one thing he wanted—oil. They did not stop to see what he really came for.

We can give God our time, our money, our service, and even our lives, but there is one thing He has told us He wants above all—our worship. Are we worshiping God? God desires our worship, for it demands our all. This again is the reason we make our time with God for Him first of all.

Returning to our picture of a loving friendship with God, we see that worship is the most intimate aspect of the friendship. Worship is a love affair with God. Worship without love is like a flame without heat, but love without worship is like a candle not lit. I like the way C. S. Lewis expressed the thought that in worship God imparts Himself to us.

Worship is how we express our love to God. We only really love someone when we love them the way they want to be loved. Jesus says, "For such people the Father seeks to be His worshipers" (John 4:23). This is what He wants.

The fourth and most significant answer to why we have a quiet time is to worship our God who deserves it and seeks it from us. (If you are hungry for more about worship at this point, skip over to Part 3 for God's "how-to.")

—— *Reflection* ——————————————

1. Since God seeks those who worship Him, how will that change the priorities of your quiet time?
2. Why is God seeking your worship? What does it mean to Him?
3. What have you learned about worship in the Old and New Testaments that can help you in your time of devotion today? Next year?
4. What is your favorite Psalm? Try repeating it to God as if it were your own.

CHAPTER SIX

From Roots to Fruits

The more I love thee with a truly gracious love, the more I desire to love thee, and the more miserable I am at my want of love.

—Puritan Prayer, *The Valley of Vision*

THE ROOTS OF THE TREE give it stability and supply the needs for growth. The deeper and larger the roots, the taller and stronger the tree. The same is true of our personal friendship with God. There are four roots that give it strength and supply its needs. The taproot is *knowing*—not merely knowledge. It is lived-out, practical, active, personal knowing. It can always grow deeper and better. Knowing this amazing God who made us like Himself is the highest of all privileges, the deepest of all mysteries. And yet, knowing Him can be the most natural of all relationships. This is what He has made possible.

The root of *enjoying* this personal God and becoming His friend is the most desirable outcome. It is the root of potential. Being called God's friend is the highest compliment. It removes all barriers, makes God reachable, puts Him first.

The root of *loving* is the most intimate part of the friendship. Marriage is the closest picture. It makes the commitment for life. It shares and listens to every thought. It simply enjoys the time together even if nothing is said. It is the root of giving and receiving. Just as the groom waits expectantly for his bride, God, too, stands at the altar waiting for His bride.

The last root is *worshiping*, which begins as a one-way experience—from us to God. It naturally flows out of our knowledge, our friendship, and our love. When we discover it is what He desires, we are delighted to give Him what means the most to Him. Yet in giving Him our worship, we find ourselves enjoying and receiving even more in return from Him. He sits on the throne worthy to be worshiped.

These lay the foundation of why we have a quiet time:

> To know Him more *fully*.
> To enjoy Him more *completely*.
> To love Him more *deeply*.
> To worship Him more *satisfactorily*.

And in each we find ourselves more secure because we are aware of how much He knows us and accepts us just as we are. We find the sheer delight of His friendship. We find the warmth and enjoyment of His love. We develop the respect and admiration of His greatness.

These roots give the quiet time its quality and value. They enable us to be inspired and motivated, make us stable and honest, and even add laughter and joy.

However, you might be saying: "I appreciate this enthusiasm and perspective, but stop telling me what a quiet time should be and help me deal with the fact that it is still hard work. What about the warts and wounds and even the diseases my quiet times endure?"

The second part of this book takes on the daily struggles of praying and Bible work. After thirty years of wrestling with these truths, I find that I am still the greatest of sinners, as Paul told Timothy, where perfect quiet times are concerned. But these truths become increasingly valuable and helpful. Let me give you the good and the bad in practical terms—a realistic discussion of the actual work and rewards of meeting with God.

PART TWO

Growth for Results

CHAPTER SEVEN

Prayer of Respect

O My God, Thou fairest, greatest, first of all objects, my heart admires, adores, loves thee, for my little vessel is as full as it can be, and I would pour out all that fullness before thee in ceasless flow.

—Puritan Prayer, *The Valley of Vision*

Real prayer comes not from gritting our teeth, but from falling in love.

—Richard Foster

PRAYER IS YOUR LIFE. It is not a time. It is a running conversation. This grabbed the disciples' attention. It was one characteristic Jesus wanted His disciples to develop so that it came as naturally to them as it did to Him. It was the only practice they actively sought to learn from Him. Take a moment to think about that—the only thing they asked Him to teach them was prayer. He must have done so much of it that they got the message without His telling them. It was not that He didn't talk about prayer, but early in their life with Him they sensed the priority of prayer.

When they asked Him to teach them to pray, He gave them what we call the Lord's Prayer in Matthew 6:9–13. He didn't provide those words because they were magic. And I don't think He expected them to say it over and over as if it alone was to be used. Instead, it was an example—a model. Its parts and principles are what He wanted them, and us, to see. The Lord's Prayer has three parts—praise, priorities, and provision.

- Give God praise—"Hallowed be Thy name."
- Keep God's priorities—"Thy kingdom come. Thy will be done."
- Seek God's provision—"Give us this day our daily bread . . . forgive us our debts . . . deliver us from evil."
- Give God praise—"For Thine is the kingdom, and the power and the glory forever."

Jesus repeats the praise to emphasize it. So praise surrounds the other two parts.

Jesus' model and other biblical examples reveal two kinds of prayer. Prayers of *respect* expressed in praise and thanksgiving, and prayers of *request* expressed in confession, petition, and intercession. When Martin Luther sought to teach his barber how to pray, he told him to begin with meditating on each phrase of the Lord's Prayer and the Ten Commandments. The purpose was to set an attitude of respect before beginning to request. Let's begin with the prayer of respect as Jesus did.

Spontaneous Thanks

Jewish tradition tells of two angels who came to earth—the Angel of Request and the Angel of Thanksgiving. They came to earth, each with a basket, to gather up the prayers of men. The Angel of Request returned to heaven, his basket overflowing with the petitions of men. The Angel of Thanksgiving also returned, with only one prayer of gratitude to God for His abundant mercies.

The Lord desires our spontaneous thanks. One of the greatest examples of this attitude is Eliezer, the servant of Abraham. Abraham sent him to find a wife for Isaac. What a job! He not only had to please Abraham, but Isaac as well. So he went to Abraham's old neighborhood to find some relatives he had never seen. But he prayed for success and God's guidance, found an eligible woman at a well, and discovered that she was the answer to his prayer. Genesis 24:26 says, "Then the man bowed low and worshiped the LORD." He gave spontaneous thanks and praise to God for answering his prayers.

The Bible is full of examples of this kind of respect, given through praise and thanksgiving. So let's turn the spotlight on this kind of praying and look at its value and place in our time with God.

A Closer Look—Thanks and Praise

My friend, Lane Adams, says, "When I get up in the morning I bump into all four walls and have to find a cup of coffee before I can get my eyes open." He claims there are two kinds of people in the morning: leapers and creepers. "And I'm a creeper," he says. Do you ever feel this way?

For some of us it is hard to get going in the morning, but whether you are a leaper or a creeper, there is something that can help make your time with God worthwhile—thanks and praise. They set the thermostat to the right temperature for personal time with God. They help kindle our emotions, help us enjoy what God gives, and help the rest of our praying—so it is best to begin with praise and thanksgiving, as Jesus suggested.

Paul said, "In everything give thanks; for this is God's will for you in Christ Jesus" (1 Thessalonians 5:18). Wherever we find ourselves, we are to give thanks for it. Even the bad, you ask? Yes, even the bad! Paul reminds us over and over to give thanks for all things, for everything that happens. When someone takes your efforts for granted, it always leaves a sour taste. Don't give God sour grapes by only offering selective thanks.

David said, "My mouth is filled with Thy praise, and with Thy glory all day long" (Psalm 71:8). Praise any time. As the opportunity arises, honor Him by giving praise. In Psalm 69:30–31, David says that *God desires thanksgiving and praise more than sacrifice.* He says, "I will praise the name of God with song, and shall magnify Him with thanksgiving, and it will please the Lord better than an ox. . . ." What he means is that God not only wanted sacrifices in the Old Testament, but a heart of praise and thanksgiving.

The Lord will receive thanks and praise from anyone giving it sincerely. Yet isn't it amazing how thankless and ungrateful we can be? I often shake my head at how much I can leave unsaid.

We are quick to notice it in others. We give something nice to a friend. He says a quick thanks and then goes off to enjoy it, and we get angry because he doesn't jump up and down over how nice we are or what a fine gift it was. We want and expect far more gratitude and praise than we get. Yet I find that I do the same thing to others—don't you? I think I am thankful and I consider saying more, but somehow I feel embarrassed or just forget.

It is especially true with those who are around us all the time and who do unselfish things for us regularly. It is so easy to take them for granted. And it is even easier to take the Lord for granted because His love, protection, provision, and forgiveness are so constant and unlimited.

This is where we must begin. It sets the tone for our time with Him.

If you want a few ideas to make your praise and thanksgiving more enjoyable, see Part 3.

The second kind of prayer is the prayer of request. The Scriptures also have much to say about this kind of prayer.

Reflection

1. What are some practical ways you can show God respect?
2. Why does God want your praise and thanksgiving more than sacrifice?
3. What difference does it make to God that we offer Him thanksgiving and praise before doing anything else in our quiet time? What difference does it make to you?
4. Why is it harder to thank and praise God than it is to ask Him for something?

CHAPTER EIGHT

Prayer of Request

I never prayed sincerely for anything but it came, at some time . . . somehow, in some shape.
—Adoniram Judson, Missionary to Burma

Captain Robert Clarke and his son James owned and sailed a fishing schooner in the North Atlantic. One night near the Arctic Circle, the darkness descended, the fog closed in, and the seas began to run high. James was at the wheel doing his best to keep the schooner on course.

His father, standing close by, reminded his son that it was about this time that their wife and mother at home was offering up her prayers for them—to the God who holds the waves in His hand. After a brief pause, Captain Clarke cried out, "All hands on deck, put a close reef in the main sail, let her run the jib—we have got to get that prayer answered!"

What does it mean to you when you know someone is praying on your behalf? What a privilege that is for us when someone we love seeks God for us!

D. L. Moody said, "Every work of God can be traced to a kneeling figure." We are all convinced that prayer works. We have all been one of those kneeling figures at one time or another—seeking God's help. But it is amazing how much we struggle with our time devoted to prayer. Why?

Prayer is hard and easy. It is usually easy if it is for our interests and desires or the normal needs and problems of life. But it gets harder when it's for those outside our circle of family and friends. Yet it is this harder area of prayer that God encourages us to pursue in the same way we pray for our own needs. When we pray as earnestly for another's needs as for our own, that is intercession. But it is difficult to keep this fresh and not merely a matter of duty or routine, especially if it is repeated regularly.

The Bible offers help for a more effective and enjoyable time of praying for requests.

Going to God for Others

First, the aim of intercession is often misunderstood. Its aim is to further God's kingdom and honor, not just to improve one's condition. How many times have we been at a prayer meeting where the things that are continually brought up for prayer are Aunt Bessie's sore back, Grandmother's broken leg, and Jim's bout with the flu? The needs are real, but how often do we forget prayer's aim—requests in line with the will of God. What is God doing in that person's life? He may have a purpose for that sore back or broken leg. Yet, we may betray a "gimme" attitude—"Lord, You have to heal Bob," "You must change the weather," "Please stop Joe from . . ." Do we want God's will or our own? What is God's will? Did anyone ask?

We *can* pray for Aunt Bessie's physical needs and glorify God, but we must pray for God's work whether or not Aunt Bessie gets well, and then give God praise regardless of the outcome. God uses trials and suffering to strengthen and bless us. In our eagerness to help, we may be asking God to remove something He intends as a blessing.

When men and women in the Bible went to God for others, their requests were not usually related to physical needs. The great examples of intercessory prayer seem to deal with the deeper needs of a person's life—spiritual needs. Let's look at two New Testament passages in Colossians and Ephesians for typical examples of kingdom-focused prayer.

Spiritual Needs

Paul had never even been to Colossae. The church was started by Epaphras, a convert of Paul's. But notice how Paul prays for the Colossians:

> For this reason also, since the day we heard of it [their salvation], we have not ceased to pray for you and to ask that you may be filled with the knowledge of His will in all spiritual wisdom and understanding, so that you may walk in a manner worthy of the Lord, to please Him in all respects, bearing fruit in every good work and increasing in the knowledge of God; strengthened with all power, according to His glorious might, for the attaining of all steadfastness and patience; joyously giving thanks to the Father, who has qualified us. . . . (Colossians 1:9–12)

When Paul intercedes for others, he prays for their spiritual needs. For the Colossians he prayed for *wisdom*—spiritual skill for daily living. He prayed for *knowledge*—understanding of the things of God. He knew they could not follow God fully until they knew what God wanted them to do. He prayed for *enlightenment*—to understand that knowledge. And he prayed for *spiritual strength*, *patience*, a *fruitful life*, and a *worthy walk*.

Now notice how he prays for the Ephesian church:

> That the God of our Lord Jesus Christ, the Father of glory, may give to you a spirit of wisdom and of revelation in the knowledge of Him. I pray that the eyes of your heart may be enlightened, so that you may know what is the hope of His calling, what are the riches of the glory of His inheritance in the saints, and what is the surpassing greatness of His power toward us who

believe. These are in accordance with the working of the strength of His might. . . . (Ephesians 1:17–19).

These are interesting requests when we remember that the Ephesian church was probably the strongest church of Paul's ministry. Paul spent more time in Ephesus than he did in almost any other place. He spent two full years teaching there, so he writes with depth. Yet he continues to pray for their spiritual needs, even though they were mature Christians. In Ephesians 3:14–19, he offers another prayer of a similar nature:

> For this reason, I bow my knees before the Father, from whom every family in heaven and on earth derives its name, that He would grant you, according to the riches of His glory, to be strengthened with power through His Spirit in the inner man; so that Christ may dwell in your hearts through faith; and that you, being rooted and grounded in love, may be able to comprehend with all the saints what is the breadth and length and height and depth, and to know the love of Christ which surpasses knowledge, that you may be filled up to all the fulness of God.

God is telling us something through Paul's prayers—that Paul's first concern was spiritual growth. He was concerned that they used what they knew.

There are three things that are important to notice about the business of going to God for others. First, Paul has some *definite* and *similar purposes* whenever he prays. Second, his prayers are always *brief.* He packs a lot into a little space, and remember, he wrote some long letters. He gets right to the point in his prayers. This indicates that he had clearly thought through what he wanted to pray. Finally, these prayers are saturated with *thankfulness.* He is thankful for the privilege and opportunity to pray for them. He is praying for God's interests.

Intercession is meeting with God about others, seeking to learn God's will for them, and then cooperating with it.

This primary aim of intercession—being in line with God's will—is further seen in the fascinating story of the first missionaries. In Acts 13:1–3, Paul and Barnabas pray and fast with some friends just before the Holy Spirit calls them to a special mission. The phrase that should catch our attention is ". . . and while they were ministering unto the Lord . . ." You see, they are not ministering *for* the Lord but *unto* the Lord. Our prayer life, whether praise, intercession, or petition, should always aim toward God's purpose. This ministers to God.

The Holy Spirit's Help

A second focus of intercession is guidance by the Holy Spirit. There will be times when God will put a specific person on our hearts, often somebody we haven't thought about in a long time. When this happens, we should definitely pray for them. Why? It would rarely be to Satan's advantage to lead us to pray, so if you sense a burden to pray for a particular person, you can be sure that it is from the Spirit of God. It is very important to pray right then. Paul says several times that having heard something about his friends, he had not ceased to pray for them.

I'll never forget hearing of a missionary in Africa who was almost bitten by a poisonous snake. As the man went to the bathhouse and stepped in the door to light the lantern, he saw something move at his feet. He squinted and turned pale. A large snake was coiled, ready to strike. All he could do was yell for help. There was only time for a flash of a prayer. The snake stood still for a second—then backed off into the corner. It should have bitten him. The man ran to get a shovel, then returned and killed it.

He was so impressed with the Lord's protection that he wrote down the incident in a prayer diary. Back in the United States several years later, he spoke to a large gathering of how God had done miraculous things on the mission field. And he shared the incident of God's protection from the snake.

After the meeting a lady approached him and said, "Sir, I am very interested in your story. When was it that God spared you from the snake?"

He said, "Well, I happen to have that recorded in my prayer diary."

She opened up her prayer diary and said, "During that time your name flashed across my mind, and it seemed so important that I prayed for your safety." They looked at their prayer diaries and it was exactly the same day.

This is a mysterious element of prayer, but a true one. God does lay needs of others on our hearts. We don't always have the opportunity to know what happened, but one day we will. So when God's Spirit places somebody on our heart, we ought to pray even if we do not know what to pray.

The Spirit as Translator

Romans 8 introduces another aspect of prayer, teaching that the Spirit of God intercedes for us with groanings. Dr. Manford Gutzke, a famous Bible scholar, used to say that he'd sense a need to pray for family members although they lived far away. "Lord, I don't know what to pray," he'd say. And then he would simply groan. He said the Spirit of God knew what to pray, because He "intercedes for us with groanings too deep for words" (Romans 8:26).

Remember, God does not require that we pray perfectly, only that we seek sincerely. We may pray wisely or foolishly but the real issue is love. God can translate our love into the proper request and pass over our foolish prayers. He even takes our groans and answers them.

Going to God for Me

What about our own needs? Petition is praying for our needs. James tells us that we have not because we ask not. We are not to pray with impure motives solely for selfish gain, but we may not have some things because we simply don't pray about them. It is proper to pray for material needs when we are unable to provide them for ourselves through our work and resources. Jesus reminds us in Matthew 6:11, 31–32, that our Father knows what needs we have for clothing and food.

It's also proper to pray for physical problems and health needs. In 2 Corinthians 12:7–9, Paul prayed for his health. He also received an answer. It was *no*. Paul's request was turned down. Why? There was a greater reason for a no answer. And once Paul knew the answer was no, he never asked again. But he knew that he could ask for it initially.

Ask for Anything

Jesus said, "Ask anything in my name and it shall be given to you." John said in the epistles, "If we ask anything according to His will, He hears us. And if we know that He hears us in whatever we ask, we know that we have the requests which we have asked from Him" (1 John 5:14–15). Jesus said in Mark 11:24, "Therefore I say to you, all things for which you pray and ask, believe that you have received them, and they shall be granted you." Notice those words, "ask anything," "ask . . . and they shall be granted you," "whatever we ask." Those sound like open doors to the vault, but on a second look we realize they all have conditions upon them, "ask anything *in my name*," "*believe* that you have received," "ask anything *according to His will*." We are to ask with faith, ask in line with God's will, and ask in His name, or ask in a way that would honor Jesus as if He Himself were asking.

Unconditional Answer

There is a prayer promise in the Scriptures, however, that does not have a condition upon it. It guarantees us an answer to every prayer, and it is found in Philippians 4:6–7. Paul writes, "Be anxious for nothing, but in everything by prayer and supplication with thanksgiving let your requests be made known to God" (v. 6). In other words, don't sweat it. Whatever is troubling you, giving you an anxiety attack, or weighing heavily on your heart, that is what you are to pray about. Whatever it is—ask!

Make the request known to God. Now the promise: "And the peace of God, which surpasses all comprehension, shall guard your hearts and your minds in Christ Jesus" (v. 7).

What does this mean? The word *guard* was a military term that described a Roman soldier holding his weapon, walking back and forth in front of an open gate so that no one could enter. Paul is saying that this is how God will guard your hearts and give you His peace. Our Father is a Father who delights to give good gifts to His children. He will actively guard your heart against whatever is troubling it. He will not allow any menacing worry to enter.

This verse commands us to ask for anything and guarantees an answer. First, we may get what we ask for, because He delights in giving us gifts, but no matter what the outcome, He definitely promises to give us His peace. This means that if we don't get what we asked for, we've got something better—satisfaction. Our hearts will be satisfied with or without our initial request, regardless of what was troubling us to begin with.

What's Behind Your Back?

How does this work?

A friend of mine, speaking to a football player at Georgia Tech, said, "Bob, I bet I can tell you what you pray before every football game."

"Well, then," Bob replied, "tell me. What do I pray before a football game?"

He said, "I bet you pray that it'll be a good game, and that the best team will win, and that nobody will get hurt."

Bob said, "Well, yeah, that's pretty much what I pray."

My friend replied, "Bob, let me ask you a question. Do you ever pray to win?"

"No, you shouldn't pray to win," Bob said. "I mean, you know, that wouldn't be fair. Besides, what if the other team has Christians and they were praying to win? You'd put God in a predicament, wouldn't you?"

"Not necessarily," said my friend. "God is sovereign. He can handle the 'who's going to win' problem. But let me ask you, do you want to win?"

"Yes, of course."

"Well, Bob, let me tell you what you're doing. You're taking the request that you really have, wanting to win, and you're putting that behind your back. Yet you're saying, 'God, I hope the best team wins and nobody gets hurt.' Also, Bob, don't you really want to be the best player on the field?"

"I guess I hadn't really thought about it that way."

So my friend concluded, "Actually, you're lying to God, because you're not telling Him what you want. You're telling Him something you think He wants you to say."

And that's Paul's point in Philippians 4.

Whatever makes us anxious—that which we really want, what's bugging us down in our hearts—to these God says, "Ask. Let it be made known. After all, I can see behind your back; I know what you really want anyway." He wants us to ask for the things that are on our hearts. He promises that He will give us His peace. And He may also give us our request.

Points That Work

There are four prayer principles from Philippians 4. First of all, *be honest* with God. Tell God what you want—what's really on your heart. It isn't normal to put off a pressing, worrisome desire or need by trying to pray for other things because you feel you are supposed to. If it is bothering you, tell God what you want. Be honest with Him. He understands.

Second, *be specific*. Many times I hear people say, "God bless the missionaries." How in the world would we ever know if God blessed the missionaries? Or we say, "God help me in this situation." Well, we might receive several different forms of help. How would we know which one was from Him? We are rarely specific enough in our praying. Paul, on the other hand, is very specific in his prayers for others. Specific prayers require more attention on our part, but they get more attention from God. He says, "in everything" make the request known.

Third, *be brief*. We don't have to try to convince or connive God. Just tell Him what you want. Martin Luther said, "The fewer the words, the better the prayer." He also said, "To have prayed well is to have studied well." Brevity takes thought. Make the request known—without begging or trying to convince.

Fourth, *be thankful*. Paul says that whatever your requests, pray and ask with thanksgiving. We know that God is going to give an answer, whether yes or no or wait. We also know that by praying we can have the unexplainable peace of God in our hearts. It is to satisfy our anxiety sometimes that we are drawn to God. And who knows, we may get the request we gave to God. Prayer always creates a new situation, so we can give thanks.

A Unique Occupation

Praying for ourselves and others is a unique work. It is like Jack Collingsworth's job as a nautical instruments technician. In the early spring, just before the ice breaks up in the Great Lakes, Jack goes on board the ships that pry open the waters of Lakes Michigan, Huron, and Erie and checks their instruments. These ships are tied up in a quiet harbor alongside a concrete dock, where they are free from any movement. In that quiet basin, he examines and corrects the compasses and other instruments used to guide the ships. Jack then gives his approval and reports his results to the captain, telling him that he can depend upon them as he starts out on his voyage.

Prayer is like that. It is anchoring ourselves in some quiet spot and letting God come aboard our lives and make the adjustments to His will which are necessary in both our lives and others as we pray. Prayer becomes a two-way street. We seek His will for others and ourselves, we tell Him our deepest needs, and He meets us where we are, as we are, and works His peace within us.

In *The Practice of the Presence of God*, Brother Lawrence said:

God lays no great burden upon us; a little remembrance
of Him from time to time, a little adoration, sometimes

to pray for His grace, sometimes to offer Him your sorrows, and sometimes to return Him thanks for the benefits He has given you. You need not cry very loud; He is nearer to us than we think.

As part of your time of devotion, meet with God in prayer. Let Him bless you and use you for His will. Talk to God and let Him talk to you. Discover how to listen to Him.

—— *Reflection* ——————————————

1. What is the focus of Paul's intercessional prayers?
2. Have you ever been dishonest in your prayers by praying for what you thought you should pray for instead of bringing before God your real requests? How did that make you feel? How did it make God feel?
3. Why do we find few examples of prayer for personal needs in the New Testament?
4. How can you apply the Holy Spirit's help as you pray for yourself and for others?

CHAPTER NINE

Hearing God's Voice

We being docile under the Word of God, then only can we
hear the Voice of God.

—John Calvin

THE FRATERNITY HOUSE was loud, as usual, but that night the Acacia House was extra loud. Four of us, Walt, Dave, Ken, and myself, had been invited to dinner by one of the members. We were asked to speak after the meal to any of the men who wanted to stay and listen.

A group of men had remained quietly at the tables, but while we were talking, the kitchen cleanup crew really went to town. They knew we were there to talk about Christ. They were doing more than just cleaning; they were having a big time cutting up. It was disturbing, but we made it through the meeting. And as we talked, one of them, Henry, said he would like to know more.

I met Henry the next day in his room, and his roommate Tim sauntered in. Tim had been on the kitchen crew the night before. In a short time, both men's hearts were opened to respond to the gospel.

Tim and Henry entered into a new relationship with God that day. We all went to dinner that evening and Henry made an unforgettable comment. He said, "Pete, we knew you were telling us the truth this afternoon."

How did they know? I could have been from a cult—or some other religion. Yet, somehow they knew that God had spoken to them. Does God speak out loud? Was it a feeling? Did these young people have some private notion about a message from God? They were right. God had spoken to them. How then does God speak to us?

God Still Speaks

Christians often speak loosely with comments like, "This morning God told me to . . ." or "The Lord said I should . . ." Some of us give the impression that God calls us on the phone with a list of instructions for the day. Yet others will say, "I've never heard God speak out loud. He never speaks to me like He does to Martha or Bill."

What really are we saying then when we claim that God spoke to us today?

God spoke out loud to many of the biblical characters. He also used dreams, visions, angels, other humans, and finally His own Son to get His message across to us. Shortly after Jesus returned to heaven and the period of the apostles came to a close, we received the conclusion of God's written Word, the New Testament. Along with the Old Testament, it became the standard of God's speaking to everyone who has lived since, and was officially confirmed by the early church fathers. God certainly has continued to do miraculous things, and He has communicated to certain individuals in special ways through the years, but His day-in and day-out words to us—whatever our circumstance—are in the Bible, His written Word.

I used to wonder why God didn't speak out loud more often and do spectacular things for all of us to see. It finally occurred to me that He has already performed the most spectacular event He had planned for planet Earth. He sent His Son to die for our sins and to be resurrected so all would know that Jesus was God in the flesh. He was the fulfillment of all of the prophecies and promises.

He is the image of the invisible God, the firstborn over all creation. For by him all things were created: things in heaven and on earth, visible and invisible, whether thrones or powers or rulers or authorities; all things were created by him and for him. He is before all things, and in him all things hold together. And he is the head of the body, the church; he is the beginning and the firstborn from among the dead, so that in everything he might have the supremacy. For God was pleased to have all his fullness dwell in him, and through him to reconcile to himself all things, whether things on earth or things in heaven, by making peace through his blood, shed on the cross. (Colossians 1:15–20 NIV)

Now the truth is before us and it calls us to have open ears. Matthew puts it this way about Jesus, "Many prophets and righteous men desired to see what you see, and did not see it; and to hear what you hear, and did not hear it" (Matthew 13:17). In other words, God brought His message to a climax in Christ, and now we must respond.

Ears That Don't Hear

There is one very important point to remember about God's recorded words. Since the living God gave them, they are *living words* (see Acts 7:38; Hebrews 4:12; 1 Peter 1:23). They are not dry letters on the page; they have life and give life to the one who wants to hear. That is why Jesus said to the scholarly intellectuals as well as the most uneducated of His day, "He who has ears, let him hear" (Matthew 11:15 NIV). He knew they all had ears, but he also knew that not everyone who has ears will listen.

When we want to understand what God has to say, then we will hear Him. The desire to hear is evidence of the Spirit's work in our hearts. This principle is emphasized in the same parable Jesus told about the workers when he said, "For whoever has, to him shall more be given, and he shall have an abundance; but whoever does not have, even what he has shall be taken away from him" (Matthew 13:12). The context of the story is Jesus speaking to the religious leader who refused to listen to His words. The application for us is that if we want to hear and understand we will be given an abundance of understanding. If we don't, we will lose even what little we have.

"This Morning God Told Me to . . ."

Now what about people who so freely say, "God told me to . . ." or "I never hear a voice." Who is right? It is possible they are both wrong and both right!

It is *not* God's practice to speak out loud to us. He can, but it is rare when He does. So, it is correct to say that we don't normally hear His voice. It *is*, however, God's practice to make His written word come alive in our minds. God wants us to read and study it with a desire to hear what He is saying to us today. He wants us to attempt to understand it so that we can put it to work in our lives; then we will hear Him speak. How? By the thoughts that form in our minds. We engage in self-talk all the time. So when we interact with God's words they become an important part of our minds and hearts. The writer to the Hebrews puts it this way:

> For the word of God is living and active and sharper than any two-edged sword, and piercing as far as the division of soul and spirit, of both joints and marrow, and able to judge the thoughts and intentions of the heart. (Hebrews 4:12)

Notice it says the word is alive. It has life. It is also active. The word *active* means literally "at work," "energy," or "power." Therefore, the word is a living power at work in our minds. What does it do? It is able to *judge*. This word means "to discern" or "to be critical." The idea is that the word discriminates and passes judgment on our thoughts and feelings. Therefore, in practice, the Lord does speak to us in the midst of our own thoughts.

As we apply the word of God to the thoughts, feelings, and desires we have toward the activities, decisions, and events of our lives, God will speak to us through His Word. The voice will be the voice of our own thoughts, but the Spirit of God will direct His Word to show us what He wants us to understand. Information or wisdom, a sense of right and wrong, correction or instruction for godly living—this is what the Word of God will speak to. Paul says it this way:

> All Scripture is inspired by God and profitable for teaching, for reproof, for correction, for training in righteousness; that the man of God may be adequate, equipped for every good work. (2 Timothy 3:16–17)

Some Safeguards

You might ask, How can I know for sure that it's God I'm hearing and not just my own thoughts? Good question! Many people are giving God credit for direction, when actually the "direction" they claim is out of character with Him.

Are there any safeguards? Yes. They are found in two crucial areas: the way we study the Bible, and how we think about the discoveries we make in our study.

Paul told Timothy, "Be diligent to present yourself approved to God as a workman who does not need to be ashamed, handling accurately the word of truth" (2 Timothy 2:15). The word *handling* comes from an old idea of cutting a straight road or path. Paul is saying that we need to know how to make a clear path of understanding for ourselves in God's Word.

Though God's words are plain, they are also profound. God wants us to be diligent students, demonstrating our desire to listen to His words for our lives. He will speak clearly for every need, hurt, doubt, or question if we pursue Him through His words. "Ask, and it shall be given to you; seek, and you shall find; knock, and it shall be opened to you," said Jesus in Matthew 7:7.

The Safeguard of Diligent Study

The first safeguard, then, is diligent Bible study. We need to do some independent thinking about God's Word. It is God's Word in our minds that enables us to grow spiritually. We can benefit from what others say, but we benefit most from our own work in the Scriptures. When our thoughts are balanced against God's Word, we can be assured of the Lord's direction.

If a thought or idea I am considering is not contrary to God's Word, I am safe in thinking about doing it. Notice what the Bible says about itself.

> Since you have in obedience to the truth purified your souls for a sincere love of the brethren, fervently love one another from the heart, for you have been born again not of seed which is perishable but imperishable, that is, through the living and abiding word of God. . . . Therefore, . . . like newborn babes, long for the pure milk of the word, that by it you may grow in respect to salvation. (1 Peter 1:22–2:2)

Peter says that new life in Christ comes through the living and abiding Word. We grow spiritually by taking in and digesting God's Word, just as we grow physically from eating and properly digesting physical food. I don't fully understand how our physical digestion system works but I know it does, because I've watched myself grow (sometimes in the wrong places!). In our spiritual lives God's Word causes us to grow in a similar manner. But there are two steps necessary for food to work its miracle. It must first be taken in, and then it must be digested.

Digesting the Food

Taking in spiritual food is done by reading and listening to God's truth; that is the easy part. Most of us have a harder time with the digestion process. Digestion breaks food down into parts that the body can use. Digestion enables the body to do something with the food.

With spiritual food, however, many of us get biblical indigestion. We hear the Bible week after week at church meetings, and we read it from time to time on our own, but we don't really seem to gain anything from it for the long run. It does not get broken down into usable parts.

Why? God gives us a clue in the book of James.

Listen Up!

Through some carefully chosen words, James shows how the truth of God can be digested (James 1:19–27). In verses 19 through 21 he tells us to prepare our hearts for God's Word in two ways. First be quick to hear, and don't be so concerned about what you want to say. Have an attentive ear so you are ready to hear God, not yourself.

Second, put aside anything that would hinder a receptive spirit. In verse 21 he refers to the "filthiness and all that remains of wickedness." This is the moral uncleanness left over from our old way of life—old habits and ways that keep us from being open to God. Our openness to God's Word is influenced by the magazines we read, the movies we see, and the attitudes we harbor. James encourages his readers to avoid the trappings of their former life and instead take on a humble attitude and receive the implanted word.

James very carefully chose this word *implanted*. As a matter of fact, it isn't found anywhere else in the Bible. It means a word that has the characteristic of a seed. It will take root and bear fruit if we are attentive and receptive.

In verses 22 through 25 James says that we are to practice the Word. We prepare our hearts to receive a word that is meant for practice. This is where the problem of spiritual indigestion occurs—in our practice. And this is why Bible reading and study fail and why we do not grow from the Word as we desire. Finally, in the last two verses (26–27), we are to prove that word by doing what it says.

The Doers and the Hearers

James's main idea is that we need to be doers of the Word and not merely hearers. In the midst of this thought, he again chooses some unusual words which tell us what it means to be a mere "hearer" and an effectual "doer."

A mere hearer of God's Word is one who deludes himself. This word *delude* is a Greek word meaning to "mislead oneself by false reasoning." James says we hear God's Word but then we deceive ourselves by wrong thinking about what we have heard.

When we hear God's Word, there are three avenues of response: how we will think, how we will feel, and how we will act. How do we reason falsely along these lines and so mislead ourselves? In our thinking, when we hear the Word of God and see its truth, it is very easy to reason that we have heard this truth before or that it doesn't really apply to us and therefore do not think further about it. We substitute those secondary thoughts for the action we should take. Thus we reason ourselves out of action!

Even more deceptive is our emotional response. We hear the Word of God and are deeply moved by what we hear. We say, "Wow, that really hit me," or, "That was a powerful message," and we feel very deeply about it. However, because we felt so strongly about it, we reason falsely by substituting our strong feelings for strong action. We let feelings stop us from acting.

The third and proper avenue is to do something about what we've heard. Activating our will is what we must do if it is to be a true response. Doing something about the Word shows that it is being digested and used in our life.

James says that the "hearer" is like the man who looks at the mirror and then goes away. He glances once and doesn't take a long look, and the result is that he forgets what he looks like. This word *forgets* means "to neglect." He sees some truth but neglects to respond.

By contrast, James discusses the doer. He says that the "doer" looks closely at himself through the mirror of God's Word and continues to do so. He has made up his mind not to become a forgetful doer, because he takes a long look at himself and what Christ wants him to be. He sees that God demands a response to His truth and determines to do it.

Diligent Bible study and active response, then, is the first safeguard in knowing God's voice from our own thoughts. The Word is necessary for your spirit, just as food is necessary for your body. Food must be taken in (studied) and digested (acted upon) before it is useful. Chapter 10 provides some brief suggestions on how to study the Bible.

The Safeguard of Careful Thinking

The second safeguard relates to thinking through the discoveries we make in our study. Joshua illustrates this safeguard of careful thinking and writes about it. God told Joshua:

> This book of the law shall not depart from your mouth, but you shall meditate on it day and night, so that you may be careful to do according to all that is written in it; for then you will make your way prosperous, and then you will have success. (Joshua 1:8)

God chose Joshua for a big job. It was bigger than anything God had asked him to do. Joshua knew the stories of the great men whom God has used—Abraham, Isaac, Israel, Joseph. And he had personally served one of the greatest leaders his people had ever known—Moses. Their greatest treasure was the Law, God's written Word. Moses had been its recipient and original recorder.

Now Joshua, a servant and military man, is called on to lead God's great nation. How is he going to do it? He must have thought he would never be as great as Moses. God, however, told him the secret of greatness, the secret of success. He told Joshua two things. First, "Just as I have been with Moses, I will be with you; I will not fail you or forsake you" (1:5). So "be strong and courageous! . . . for the LORD your God is with you wherever you go" (1:9). This was the secret of God's *presence*.

The second secret God gave to Joshua was just as simple: Get into My words and let My words get into you (1:8). This is how you will develop strength in your faith. Know My Word and do it. You know how to do that, don't you, Joshua? By meditating on My Word so it will not depart from you. If you do this, Joshua, I guarantee that your way will be prosperous and successful. This was the secret of God's *success,* believing His presence and thinking His thoughts.

God's promised presence to Joshua is also our promise. Jesus said, "I will never desert you, nor will I ever forsake you" (Hebrews 13:5). The promised success of God is also our promise. Jesus said, "If you abide in Me, and My words abide in you, ask whatever you wish, and it shall be done for you" (John 15:7).

Our second safeguard is based on the latter part of God's secret to Joshua. God's Word not only guards against wrong thinking about His Word, and, consequently, His will, but it also blesses our lives. God told Joshua that *meditation* would help him to do His will. This in turn would make him prosperous and insure success. Psalm 1:1–3 reinforces this truth:

> How blessed is the man who does not walk in the counsel of the wicked, nor stand in the path of sinners, nor sit in the seat of scoffers! But his delight is in the law of the LORD, and in His law he meditates day and night. And he will be like a tree firmly planted by streams of water, which yields its fruit in its season, and its leaf does not wither; and in whatever he does, he prospers.

Meditation brings God's blessings. And meditation that motivates us to do God's Word will always bring God's prosperity and God's success as Joshua and David tell us.

Exactly what is meditation? There are two Old Testament words for meditating. One means "to moan or utter," or, "to speak for." The other word means "to study," "to muse," or, "to think about." They are synonyms, and the ideas in their raw form give us a clue as to what the Hebrew people meant by meditation. They did not just stand around thinking about God's Word, they actually uttered it. They talked about it to themselves.

Have you ever caught yourself talking to yourself? When we become aware that we are discussing something out loud, that is meditation in its truest form. There is a good reason for this. Talking out loud holds our concentration.

Lessons from a Cow

The best way to explain meditation is by describing how cows "chew the cud." When a milk cow saunters out in the morning, she eats grass for a couple of hours like a mowing machine. She walks all over the pasture, chewing and swallowing the grass into her first stomach compartment. When it starts to get hot, about 10 o'clock in the morning, she walks over to a shade tree and lies down.

She then brings up one of the little balls of grass that she had swallowed. She begins to re-chew this small ball of grass called a cud. She chews and chews on it. She will chew the cud until she knows she has gotten every bit of taste out of it; then she swallows all of it into a second stomach compartment. There it is digested and processed into her bloodstream. The work of chewing makes the digestion easy. This nourishes her and helps her produce milk.

Meditation for us is the same kind of spiritual thought digestion. Thinking about the things of God simply allows His words to fill our minds. Meditation is taking those thoughts and words in our minds and chewing on them *until* they become thoughts that can nourish us, thoughts on which we can grow. It takes effort.

Another way to look at meditation is as a type of analyzing. It's like taking a prism and letting light shine through it and then turning it and looking at every angle to see the beautiful light it produces. Or looking at a diamond and checking every facet of it, every angle, studying its beauty—that is meditation.

Read Psalm 104 as an example of King David's meditating on creation.

Working It Out

But not only is it chewing or analyzing—*meditation is action.* It's making words into thoughts and then thoughts into action. It is *mental planning* with definite action in mind for accomplishing a job. Andrew Murray described it this way, "Hold the word of God in your heart until it has affected every phase of your life."

Pulling it all together—meditation is prolonged thought about the works, and ways, and purposes, and promises of God, with the aim of doing something about those thoughts to honor God. Remember, meditation is not just dreaming about our own thoughts; it's not daydreaming. The Bible does not teach the believer to meditate or engage in mental reflection for its own sake (such as transcendental meditation). This can be very dangerous indeed because there are no safeguards. Rather the psalmist said, "My soul is satisfied as with marrow and fatness, and my mouth offers praises with joyful lips. When I remember Thee on my bed, I meditate on Thee . . ." (Psalm 63:5–6). The purpose of meditation is to *change our conduct* and *renew our minds* so that we honor God.

Practice That Profits

Finally, there are four guidelines for profitable meditation. First, *emphasize different words.* Use, for example, John 16:23. Jesus says, "If you shall ask the Father for anything, He will give it to you in My name." Stop and emphasize *ask.* "*Ask* the Father for anything." The idea is that I've got to ask before I get my request. It won't come by wishing. "Ask the *Father* for anything," emphasizing the next key word. I may not get my request by talking to my neighbor or my senator, but the *Father* is ready now to hear my request and respond to it. "Ask the Father for *anything,*" emphasizing another word. The Lord does not limit what I can ask. I can ask *anything.* The idea is to chew on each word and analyze it so that you get the full understanding and nourishment from each thought.

Second, *put the verse in your own words*. For example, on that particular verse we might say something like, "Lord, thank You that I can tell You all that is in my heart and bring every request to You." This is paraphrasing it into our language. This gives us another view. After writing it down in our own words, we can see how much we have understood.

Third, *ask questions*. In this particular passage, we might ask, Who is Jesus talking to? What is He saying to them? Why is He telling them this? When is this happening? Does the time make any difference? Is He telling me something new about prayer? Where should I pray? Where have I failed to pray? When should I pray? Why does God say I should pray? How should I go about praying? These are the simple questions: who, what, when, where, why, and how. What we want to do is come at the truth from one avenue and then another. Some of those questions may not yield much, but one of them will get to the main idea and produce key insights regarding that particular verse.

Finally, *apply the fruit of the meditation*. Again, ask questions, like, What truth is here for me to do? First Timothy 4:15 says, "Take pains with these things; be absorbed in them, so that your progress may be evident to all." The idea is "take pains," practice, attend to, be diligent in. What's this telling me that I need to know? Is there a practice that I should begin, or a habit I ought to eliminate? Whatever God brings to your mind, do it!

Back to Basics

This takes us back to our original question. What do we mean when we say, "The Lord told me to . . ."? If we have been diligently studying His Word, chewing and analyzing what we have read, we will know that God has spoken. We can legitimately say, "The Lord told me to do this." Sometimes these thoughts from the Lord come right at the time of our study; other times the Lord speaks to us days, weeks, maybe months later about something we have meditated on. But we can be assured that if we study and meditate, God will speak to us. He will speak to us with our own mental voice, but it will be His word to us. His voice in our thinking will always be in accordance with the written Word. It will *never* be at odds with the Scripture (1 Corinthians 2:10–16).

Meditate Consistently

Try to meditate regularly on at least one verse a week. And, of course, everyone's schedule is different, but according to author Jim Downing, one of the best times to meditate is at night before going to sleep. This is when our subconscious takes over. In his fascinating book called *Meditation*, Downing discusses the findings of his in-depth study on how the subconscious works at night, how it takes over from the conscious mind, and what the Word of God can do in your subconscious. Meditation helps sort out problems and allows you to wake up with the Lord's answers on your mind. The early morning is also a good time for meditating, if only for five or ten minutes. The time of day is not most important. The important matter is that we do it.

Stop Those Runaway Thoughts

Another unique value to meditating is the dam effect. Many of us struggle with run-on thinking and racing thoughts. These things create ruts in our minds. Whenever we start thinking about our problems, remember we have probably thought about it the same way before. When rain water runs off a bare hill, it digs ruts. All the rain that falls on that hill will eventually follow those same ruts until deep gullies are formed. This is what happens in our thought life. We build gullies or single-track thinking. These gullies develop into sloppy thinking patterns. A thought comes into our minds and we're tempted to sin. Before we stop it, we let that thought go down the same old gully toward sin. Something can stimulate our thinking and we go right down the gully of jealousy, or the gully of lust, or the gully of self-pity.

How do we keep these gullies from working against us? We build flood gates or dams. Meditation helps build a dam across a particular gully. It can then help us rechannel the thought or problem into right thinking—truth. As we look for the Word of God that applies to a certain area and meditate on it, it builds a dam that can stop the habit of wrong thinking. The Word of God can help us gain victory over worry for example (Philippians 4:6–9). It can also help us relieve tension and anxiety. Isaiah said, "The steadfast of mind Thou wilt keep in perfect peace, because he trusts in Thee" (Isaiah 26:3). That is one reason David said, "Let the words of my mouth and the meditation of my heart be acceptable in Thy sight, O LORD" (Psalm 19:14). (Many of these ideas come from *Changing Your Thought Patterns*, by George Sanchez.)

Meditation—Memorization

The greatest aid to meditation is memorization. Memorizing Scripture becomes the source of storage so we can meditate whenever we need it. Memorizing gives us a bank account from which to draw when we are lonely, grieving, confused, hurting, or when we just have extra time. Memorize different verses which relate to a variety of needs. Do this as you drive or walk or clean the house.

Caution—Two Holes Ahead

There are two cautions for memorizing. First, it is easy to be *lazy* and undisciplined about God's Word. Second, it is easy to become *legalistic* about it. We can memorize for the sake of memorizing. Remember, the ultimate aim of meditation is action. It is not enough to read God's Word, though we need to read it. But read it, memorize it, study it, and meditate on it.

We come back again to the reason for a quiet time and why we meditate during our time of devotion. It helps us listen to God. It is for Him far more than us. And God wants us to know Him and become intimate with Him.

The Hebrew word for "pray" literally means "to cause to meditate." When an Israelite spoke of praying he was also referring to meditation. The idea is communicating with a person and thinking deeply about him. It is what we call communion—a deep common union as two friends enjoy each other.

Does God still speak? Yes, through His Word. We are assured that it is His voice when we study His Word diligently and meditate on it thoroughly. He waits to speak to us every time we will listen.

Detecting God's Voice

Peter Lord, a Baptist minister, wrote in *Fullness* magazine about hearing God's voice. He said that God has never talked to him in an audible voice. However, God was teaching him to be sensitive to His inner voice, so that he will hear and obey Him. He went on to say that in his experience he could tell when a thought was the Lord's inner voice by applying these principles:

1. It did not contradict Scripture.
2. It was not rushed or in a hurry, yet persistent.
3. It was soft, not loud.
4. It was specific and clear.
5. The result would bring glory to Him.
6. It brought peace and not confusion in his own thoughts.

God can speak directly to us or He can speak to us through friends or through people in authority over us, but He usually speaks to us through His Word. J. I. Packer said that for many Christians "their basic mistake is to think of guidance as essentially an inward prompting of the Holy Spirit, apart from the written Word" (*Knowing God*). The Holy Spirit does speak to us, but always in harmony with the Word. His speaking is one of the mysteries of meeting with God. We have no control over when He may speak, but we are responsible to listen to God from His Word.

——— *Reflection* ————————————————

1. How does God speak to you? Can you know for sure when it is He who is speaking?
2. How can you trust your own thoughts?
3. What are a few of the benefits of meditating?
4. What role does meditation play in your devotional life? What part should it have? How can you do it better?

CHAPTER TEN

Getting into God's Word

It is very certain that we cannot attain to the understanding of Scripture, either by study or by the intellect. Your first duty is to begin by prayer.

—Martin Luther

RAMAD WAS THE MOST dangerous man in all of India. His gang attacked, plundered, and terrified the remote villages of the area. He was wanted dead or alive. While ransacking a small home in one of these villages, he found a small black book. At first he started to throw it away, but he noticed that the paper was very thin and just the right size for roll-your-own cigarettes. Each evening after a meal Ramad would relax with a smoke. He would take out the little book, tear a page out and fold it over for the tobacco. One evening while folding the paper he noticed the writing was in his own language. So each evening after eating, he would read a page of the little book and then smoke it. One evening he knelt down and asked Jesus to forgive his sins and to be his Lord and Savior. The small, black book was the Bible.

He turned himself over to the police, much to their surprise, and turned from a bandit to a prisoner for Christ. The prison became Ramad's mission field where he led many other prisoners to Jesus. God's Word made the change in his life.

We all have felt the impact of God's Word at some time, but why is it that other times it seems to have no impact at all? How does the Word affect our lives? How much of it do we need to know or study in real depth? Is there a difference between Bible study and meeting with God? Is one more important than the other?

Why Study?

To answer the questions and frustrations we have all felt, I want to look again at why we study the Bible.

Spiritual growth occurs in direct proportion to our intake of the Scriptures. Think about that for a moment. Bible study results in spiritual growth and spiritual competence. Spiritual growth makes us more like Christ. Spiritual competence equips us to do His work.

We know it's for spiritual growth because Peter tells us that we need to long for the pure milk of the Word, that by it we may grow up in our salvation (1 Peter 2:2). We know it is for spiritual competence from Paul's word to Timothy. "Be diligent to present yourself approved to God as a workman who does not need to be ashamed, handling accurately the word of truth" (2 Timothy 2:15). Paul goes on to tell Timothy that the reason we need to study the Scriptures and handle them accurately is because the Scriptures are inspired by God and "profitable for teaching, for reproof, for correction, for training in righteousness" (2 Timothy 3:16). They are profitable for teaching us truth. They are profitable for reproof—for pointing out our sins and blind spots. They are profitable not only for pointing out what's wrong, but showing us what to do to correct it. They are also profitable for righteous living—living like Jesus day by day. Paul adds a final thought: all of this is for the purpose "that the man of God may be adequate, equipped for every good work" (3:17). And God has already prepared good works for us to do (Ephesians 2:10).

The Word of God equips us to do those things. So Bible study must be a priority.

A Personal Message

God gave the Scriptures as a very personal message to you and to me. He had us in mind when He had them written. To be like Christ and to be useful for Him only comes from knowing Him and pleasing Him. That's why we study the Scriptures, so we can get to know Him and please Him. There are a lot of people, even great theologians, who know far more about the Bible than we will ever know, and yet they do not know the Person behind the Bible. I'm not saying that they're not believers, I simply mean they're not getting personally involved with God.

It pleases God if we handle His Word accurately, for it shows our commitment to Him. We want to become so accustomed to God's Word that we are comfortable with it. As a matter of fact, Paul tells us in Colossians 3:16, "Let the word of Christ richly dwell within you." *Dwell* means that the Word of God should be at home in our lives in such a way that we could sit down with it just like we do with someone in our own home. We feel comfortable enough to take our shoes off, lean back in a soft chair, and enjoy ourselves. We can be as natural when we listen to God through His Word as two people having an intimate conversation in front of a fireplace on a cold day.

Ground Rules of Accuracy

To grow from our study of God's Word, a few ground rules of Bible study must be followed. First, and most importantly, we must be committed to study the Scriptures. When we make a commitment to the Word of God, we commit ourselves to meeting with Him.

Second, we must learn to be good at Bible study. We should be committed to doing it well. We should learn to handle the Scriptures accurately. Studying the Bible well comes through practice, like anything we want to do well. Do it right. Work with a Bible study method and learn how to see what is in the Word for you. Determine the meaning and discover how to make it work for you.

Third, don't lose sight of the method's values. The method can otherwise become dull. Using a method to study the Scriptures enables us to begin to think for ourselves and not be dependent on other people. This does not mean that we shouldn't refer to the insights of experts. Just resist the temptation to run to an expert with every difficult passage. A good method, if pursued, will be profitable and will help us learn to think for ourselves.

No Commentaries?

One of the first courses I had to take at seminary was Bible study methods. In that course, we had to study the Scriptures alone, without looking at any commentary whatsoever during the course. There were the answers on the shelf across the library—temptation at the doorstep. We were asked to explain what we thought a passage meant, even though we may have been wrong. Only after the assignment were we allowed to get the experts' views.

This course was designed to show us that when we compared the experts' views with our own, we had discovered many of the same things. It might not have been stated as well, but we had discovered the same truths by ourselves. This gave me a measure of confidence to find answers in Scripture. I still seek advice and read commentaries, but I've learned to think for myself and not rely entirely on others for my answers. You can do the same.

Deep Insights

Each of us needs a study method—a tool for discovery. Have you ever found yourself in a Bible study group, and someone says he saw an interesting truth but you didn't even come close? Then you ask yourself, "How come I didn't see that?" It is probably because he has trained himself to look at the Scriptures more carefully. It's very important to see in depth. Seeing deeply is a matter of practice. It can give a glimpse of something that opens up the whole truth. It comes from learning to observe. The principles of observation can be learned. (For more help on this topic, see the list of Bible study aids at the end of this chapter.)

Spotting the Truth

FBI personnel, particularly treasury agents, are experts at spotting counterfeit bills. However, in their training they are never given a counterfeit bill—only the real thing. They are trained to become experts on real currency. Then they can spot a suspect bill with ease because they know the real bill so well. This is a fine example of trained observation.

Our aim is to be God's treasury agents. We want to know the difference in the real truth and the half truth. To do so takes work in the details.

Catching the Half-Truth

A good study method can enable us to evaluate what we see and develop personal discernment. This is important because many people say things about the Scriptures that aren't fully true. One example can be found in the popular old song, "Trust and Obey." One stanza says, "While we do His good will, He abides with us still, and with all who will trust and obey." This could lead some to the idea that if we fail to trust Him or do His will, God will not be with us. Not true! We all sin and fall, but "He Himself has said, 'I will never desert you, nor will I ever forsake you'" (Hebrews 13:5). It is still a wonderful song and I will always enjoy it; however, I know that it is not completely accurate. Studying the Scriptures can provide discernment for half-truths and incomplete truths that could lead to discouragement or wrong thinking.

In Hebrews 5:14 Paul says, "Solid food is for the mature, who because of practice have their senses trained to discern good and evil." The Scriptures can help train our sense of discernment—what is right and what is wrong. Many of the cults today are so deceptive because their teaching is close to the truth but not right on the mark. The Word helps us evaluate what others say about the Scriptures.

Having a Ball

Another value of studying the Scriptures is the fun of personal discovery. When we find something for ourselves that nobody ever told us before, it is fun. Discovering truth on our own is a great motivator. It lets us know that God wants to speak directly to us through His Word. He will still speak through others, but He will also speak clearly to us. This is the exciting part of Bible study. We may not find something new every day, but we can discover new things regularly if we keep at it.

For a Fast Start

One very effective method is the 3 x 5 method; three chapters each day and five on Sunday enables you to cover the whole Bible in one year. After each reading write down two things: what does this say to me, and how can I use this today?

A Better Love Life

The Word gives us the chance to learn more love—love for our Lord. Seeing His patience and forgiveness firsthand strengthens our love of Jesus. Paul says it is the love of Christ that compels us. Not our love for Him, but His love for us. John also reminds us, "This is love: not that we loved God, but that he loved us and sent his Son as an atoning sacrifice for our sins" (1 John 4:10 NIV). Remember, it is a personal Word—His Word—to you. He had you and me in mind when He wrote it. He knew us before the foundation of the world. It is His love letter to us.

Four-Way Stop

Stop from time to time to remember these four important principles about Bible study.

1. Bible study is *your* work. You're not doing it for anybody else. You're doing it for yourself. Remember in high school when the first question asked after an assignment was given went something like this: "How much do you want us to do?" We want to know how much we have to do to get a good grade. When studying the Bible, we are also tempted to ask ourselves

how much we need to do. When I asked that question once, my professor said, "You're not studying for me. Learn to study for a lifetime, not for a course."

2. Bible study is *not routine* work, but a process into which we grow. It is dynamic—it changes, develops, gets better, and even ebbs and flows with life. It is different from day to day. In all honesty, some days won't seem to produce much, but stick with it anyway. It won't be dry for long.

3. It's *lifetime* work. It's something we'll never stop doing. We'll never retire from knowing the Lord! God will always continue to teach us more and more about Himself. He will take us into deeper and greater knowledge, if we let Him.

4. Bible study is *challenging* work. What you get out of it is what you put into it. We have to decide. What kind of Christians do we want to be? Once we've decided that we want to be the best Christians we can be, then we must ask ourselves, How much are we willing to pay?

Once we realize that it's our work, that no one is going to do it for us, that it is not a dull routine, but something that we develop, that it's a lifetime responsibility, and we can never become complacent, that it's a challenging task, we have to pay the price—only then we can expect dividends. I've got to work hard to reap the rewards that God promises. I have to step out in faith and try. The bee that makes honey, remember, is not the bee that hangs around the hive.

Three Aids to Bible Study

What do we need to know about Bible study to get started in a meaningful way? First of all we need to back away from our Bible study to get an overview, a bird's eye view of the Scriptures. Get the big idea first; avoid getting lost in the details. We do need to work with the details, but those details are meaningless until we get a big picture.

It's like a friend of mine who visited another friend in New York City. The visitor drove around the city, but soon got lost among all those huge buildings. So he asked his friend to show him the way to the Empire State Building. They went to the Empire State Building, took an elevator to the top, and went out on the observation deck. He looked all over the city from all four sides and said, "Okay, now I understand where we were and where I want to go." He went back down to the busy streets and never got lost again. He finally understood where to go because he got an overview of the city. We need to do that in our Bible study.

Overview Helps

There are several helps that can assist with an overview: (1) a wall chart (see charts by John C. Witcomb, Jr. or Irving Jensen), (2) a survey book (see your local Christian bookstore), (3) a commentary with book outlines, or (4) a study Bible with book outlines. Make reference to these aids before you begin so that you can put the pieces into perspective.

The Camel's Context

A second aid to Bible study is the need to study the context. A single verse in isolation will very often give an incorrect picture. For example, Jesus said, "It is easier for a camel to go through the eye of a needle, than for a rich man to enter the kingdom of God" (Matthew 19:24). We can't take that literally, because it was not intended to be taken literally. It was an illustration given as a figure of speech. Looking at nearby paragraphs helps us understand Jesus' words.

Different Scenarios

A third aid is the need to understand the different types of literature in the Bible. They have to be studied differently. The book of Proverbs cannot be studied like Romans. The book of Daniel cannot be studied like Matthew. These books are written in different styles of literature. Two excellent books that help with knowing how to study different types of biblical literature are *How to Study the Bible for Yourself* by Tim LaHaye and *Understand* by Walter Henrichsen.

Four Goals in Bible Study

What are the goals for Bible study? Goals are best stated as questions, and four good questions relating to Bible study are:

1. What does it say?
2. What does it mean?
3. How does it apply?
4. What does it tell me about Christ?

Each goal or question must be answered. We have to think clearly about what God is saying to us. We have to think deeply about what it means to us. We have to think broadly about what we can do with it. Many accomplish the first goal. Fewer accomplish the second. Fewer still achieve the third goal. Yet most forget the fourth goal all together.

Application is one of the biggest problems in Bible study. Applying what we've learned will be examined more thoroughly in the next chapter. It is by far the most neglected part of our Bible study. Satan is happy when we study the Scriptures but fail to apply them. We may recognize that we need to confess a sin, but then we fail to say when we're going to do it or how we're going to do it, so our awareness does not change a thing. Before we know it the week has gone by, we've gotten into something else and forgotten all about dealing with the sin. God's Word is meant to be acted on—not heard and forgotten.

Finally, we come back to our overall premise that all Bible study and devotional time is to lead us to the Person—Jesus.

I have not attempted to write about the "how-to" of Bible study. We would need more than one chapter, and there are too many good books available on the subject. Below are some of the best "how-to" Bible study books currently available.

Hendricks, Howard G., and William D. Hendricks. *Living By the Book*. Chicago: Moody Press, 1996.
Jensen, Irving. *Enjoy Your Bible*. Chicago: Moody Press, 1963.

LaHaye, Tim. *How to Study the Bible for Yourself.* Rev. and exp. Eugene, Ore.: Harvest House, 1998.

Longman III, Tremper. *Reading the Bible with Heart and Mind.* Colorado Springs: NavPress, 1997.

Wald, Oletta. *The Joy of Discovery.* Minneapolis: Augsburg, 1975.

—— *Reflection* ————————————————

1. What do you like most about your Bible study method? Least?
2. How do you learn to apply the truth of Scripture to your own experience?
3. Because Bible study equips us to do works of service, what difference does it make that we spend quality time in God's Word?

CHAPTER ELEVEN

Maintaining the Quality

Finally, brothers, whatever is true, whatever is noble, whatever is right, whatever is pure, whatever is lovely, whatever is admirable–if anything is excellent or praiseworthy–think about such things.

—Philippians 4:8 NIV

AN AIRLINE PILOT FLYING over the southeastern United States called a local tower and said, "We are passing over at 35,000–give us a time check."

The tower said, "What airline are you?"

"What difference does it make? I just want the time," replied the pilot.

The tower responded, "Oh, it makes a lot of difference.

"If you are British Air or Lufthansa, it is 1600.

"If you are United or Delta, it is 4 o'clock.

"If you are Southern Airways, the little hand is on the 4 and the big hand is on the 12.

"If you are Skyway Airlines–it's Thursday."

If you have ever flown on your regional airlines, you know the frustration of late planes and wasted time. This is often true of our time with God. We put in our minutes, but it doesn't seem to get us what we expect.

Simple and Powerful

Christian psychiatrist and author Paul Meier once told me, "Experience proves that most time is wasted, not in hours, but in minutes. A bucket with a small hole in the bottom gets just as empty as a bucket that is deliberately kicked over."

Have you ever floundered in your devotional life because you didn't have a regular time? You did a little here and a little there, but it just didn't seem to work out.

This frustration is common, and it can be solved by understanding two simple but powerful principles.

The Principle of Timing

The principle of *timing* is simple—obvious—yet so much misery over meeting with God begins and ends right here! Have you ever heard anybody say, "If you don't meet God in the morning, He won't be with you the rest of the day"? Feel guilty? Join the crowd. Or have you ever heard anyone say, "I had two hours in prayer with the Lord this morning; it was just great!" Again we walk away feeling low and guilty. We know our prayer lives do not quite measure up.

Each of these issues relates to understanding the principles that are involved in the timing of the devotional life.

Feelings of guilt come for many reasons. Some of them may be valid, but they may also come from misunderstanding this principle of the time we spend meeting with God. Stop and remember that the basis for the devotional life is time *for* God—for your relationship with Him. It's a time to know and to love Him as a person—as a friend sitting next to us—only a whole lot better. He thinks, chooses, feels—and He's made us the same way. We can love Him, even though we cannot see Him.

The Highest Aim

Old Testament scholar Dr. Bruce Waltke recently said, "After all my studies of the Scripture from an Old Testament standpoint, I'm finding that my highest desire is to be like the psalmist in Psalm 73:25, where he says, 'I want to get to the place where

I love God more than anything else in the world.' That is my highest aim. I'm not there yet, but that's what I want." This speaks to where we are and yet it is so easily lost. Our aim is to love God more than anyone or anything else. We may be a long way from achieving that goal, but we can grow toward it as we meet with Him.

You Be the Judge

A devotional is a time devoted to a person. We'll never have a friendship with a person just by talking with him in the morning. It simply isn't true that God is not going to be with us just because we didn't meet with Him on a particular morning. This is a very limited view of God. A relationship does not solely depend on the quantity of time spent. The quality of time is equally important. Thus while the amount of time is important, it is more important to evaluate the use of our available time each day.

Never let someone else's experience be the guide by which you judge your own. We can gain from others' experience, but it is *your* relationship with Him that matters, not someone else's. We will not be asked if our life measured up to Sam's or Ruth's.

Once you have decided that developing a friendship with God is a priority, set a *definite* time to develop that friendship. The time you set becomes your standard. After it is established and practiced, only then be flexible with necessary changes. Make a definite time to meet with the Lord, no matter when—morning, noon, or night.

Avoid Pitfalls

Setting a definite time enables us to avoid several pitfalls. By being definite we avoid the pitfalls of *laziness* and *legalism*. People can quickly fall into these two extremes. One extreme says, "I know God loves me so much that He accepts me no matter what I do." In other words, "I can be a little lazy about what I do." On the other hand, some of us are still so unsure about God's love for us that we are working, working, working all the time to make sure God will keep loving us. We have become legalistic. We know this has happened when we feel overly guilty when we miss one day with Him.

God has said, "I have loved you with an everlasting love" (Jeremiah 31:3). He will never love us more than He loves us right this moment. He cannot love us more. He is never going to love us any more than He loves us right now because He loves without holding back. What a God! What a friend! His love for us and its certainty is the only motivation that can change laziness and insecurity. Setting a regular time will fan the fire of that motivation.

Establishing a definite time can also help us avoid the pitfall of *inconsistency*. Being inconsistent is probably the most common problem of all. Having a set time in our schedule and working to meet that schedule helps us to be consistent. When we don't, the attitude soon becomes, "Well, I met with Him a couple of times this week, and I will meet with Him a couple times next week." Before we know it we begin to miss entire weeks, and the warmth of our relationship cools.

A set time can also help us avoid the pitfall of *interruptions*. If we have set the right time, an appropriate time, we won't run into those interruptions that spoil our enjoyment of being with Him. How often have we started reading our Bible or praying, and somebody knocks on the door? Little Johnny comes in and says, "Daddy, look at this bug I found." "Okay, son," you say politely, "thank you very much." Or, "Daddy, can you please come here and turn the light on for me?" Murphy's Law applies in the spiritual dimension too: If anything can interrupt your quiet time with God, it will. So there will always be interruptions, but we can avoid many of them if we set the right time and the right place.

Inside Problems

Not only are there external interruptions but internal ones as well. We're all prone to wander away from God. Our nature is bent toward sin, and our tendency is to stray away from God.

Therefore, setting a definite time can help deal with these problems in our lives.

One of the biggest internal interruptions is the nagging urge to clean up our cluttered desk—to clear up unfinished work. How many times have we sat down to read the Scripture or pray and noticed an unfinished letter, a newspaper, a magazine, or a project? The next thing we know we've used up all the time we planned to spend with the Lord because we thought we would finish up one more little thing. We need to set a time when we are least likely to be distracted by things we need to do. Do not plan to study or pray right before you walk out the door for the day. My wife is most practical when it comes to a cluttered desk. She brings a big towel into our study room and covers her desk. She is not distracted by "to do" lists or unfinished projects staring her in the face. Better yet, you may want to change the place. When you set a time, always anticipate interruptions. They will come and destroy or dilute our time with God.

Jesus met alone with God. Mark 1:35 tells us, "In the early morning, while it was still dark, He arose and went out and departed to a lonely place, and was praying there." Jesus often went out to be alone, but it was hard for Him to get alone. He sometimes had to get up long before everyone else, because He was surrounded all the time by people and their needs. David also had set times. He mentions them in Psalms 5:3 and 59:16. He also ordered set times for praise and thanksgiving at the temple (1 Chronicles 23:28–32).

Trying to Be Somebody Else

When we set a definite time to be with God we must be realistic. I'll never forget the story of John Wesley. He was an itinerant preacher, and if ever there was anyone who epitomized the itinerant preacher, it was John Wesley. During his ministry he covered more than 250,000 miles on horseback or by carriage. And whether he was at home or away from home, when it was 10:00 p.m., he would excuse himself by telling his host that he had to go to bed because he had an appointment to keep at 4:00 the next morning.

I remember hearing that and thinking, "Wow, that must be the secret of what it means to become a man of God." So I decided that I would do what Wesley did. I was going to really get with it, but since 4:00 A.M. seemed rather early, I decided to try 5:00. I set the alarm and got up right at 5:00. I must have bumped into all four walls before I figured out how to get to the door. Out the door safely, I moved into the study and sat down at my desk to have this fabulous meeting with God. Then I opened up my Bible and dug in. The next thing I remember was waking up—at 8:00.

I decided not to let that discourage me. So, I thought I would try 5:30. The next morning I got up at 5:30 and told myself that it was a little easier to get up. I opened my Bible and started writing. The next thing I knew, I had scribbled down to the bottom of my page.

My wife started gently telling me that the real problem was not when I got up but rather when I went to bed. This was why Wesley had a disciplined time of going to bed. The point is that we must be realistic about our schedule and sleep needs, and we must decide for ourselves the *best time* to meet with God and then set our schedule accordingly. I say this for two reasons. Not only is it the best time for us, but it becomes the best time we have for God. It is time we are giving to Him, and we want to give Him our best. Whenever it is, whatever we have for Him, it makes no difference, because it's a relationship.

Eighteen Super Minutes

When I first began to fall in love with my wife, we were students at the University of Texas. I began to seek out every possible way to be with Harriet. This presented a problem, however, because I was working and carrying a full class load. If I knew she was on campus when I was, I would look for her. Even if I only had five minutes between classes, I would find her and spend time with her. It was still hard to find enough time because I worked seven nights a week at the State Capitol. I got off at eleven thirty, and it took me exactly twelve minutes, using every shortcut, to get to her sorority house. We had eighteen super minutes together before I had to leave at midnight. On the weekends we would spend as much time together as we could.

Just as my life began to focus on being with Harriet whenever I could because I was devoting myself to one person, so also my meeting with God becomes a point of focus because it is a time devoted to the person of God. What my dating life illustrates is that the amount of time I had with Harriet was not uppermost in my mind. We took whatever we could find. We just wanted to be together.

Busy Schedules? God Knows

God knows how busy we are. He is saying to us, just as I was saying to Harriet, "If eighteen wonderful minutes is all you have to give, that's what I want. If you can only stop by for five minutes, please come for five, because I love you and want to be with you."

We can't put our friendship with God into a time slot any more than we can put our friendship with our mates in one. We take every moment they will give us. Even better, we have God with us all day. We are never separated from Him (Psalm 139:7–12).

Even though Harriet and I only had eighteen minutes an evening with each other, we spent all day Saturday and Sunday together. We knew you could not have a growing, deepening friendship with only eighteen minutes. The quality of time is the most important factor, but quantity of time follows closely behind.

God knows when we have interruptions, important meetings, deadlines, sick children, doctor appointments. . . . We may only have ten minutes to give to the Lord; but most of us say, "I can't get anything out of ten minutes," so we don't have it at all. This is the root of the problem. Rather than seeing time with

God as moments with a friend, we see it as time during which we accomplish something only for ourselves. We need to *give* those minutes, rather than say, "I can't *get* anything."

If we gain this attitude, the quantity will begin to rise to its own level of importance. The more I love my wife, the more time I want to spend with her. The more you grow in your love for God, by using the many short moments you have to express that love, the more your time with Him will grow. You will want to spend more time with Him and not do it simply because you feel an obligation.

We will not deepen our relationship with the Lord, of course, if we have only ten minutes each day. We need those longer times as well. Yet, the more we give in the short, tight times, the easier it is to give when we have longer times with Him. It is when we keep that definite time with the Lord that the longer, less frequent times become more meaningful. Please don't misunderstand. Be careful to take as much time as you can, but do it with a heart that wants to be there.

The Mind-Set Principle

Once you've set a definite time, keep that time the same. It is much better to set a time and keep that time the same every day than to set one time on Monday, another time on Wednesday, and another time on Friday. Unless your schedule demands that, and sometimes it may, set a standard time at the same hour daily. There is a very good reason for this.

Our minds work in patterns and structure. When we start doing something at a set time every day—sitting down at our desks, or going to work, or getting on that plane—our minds go into a gear, or a channel. We begin to function and produce according to the mind-set we develop for that time. We are creatures of habit. Thus, having the same time for meeting with God will move us into spiritual gear. Our minds will be receptive for spiritual things at that time.

Now for some whose schedules change frequently, or whose work shift changes from time to time, consistency of time becomes harder. However, God in His grace knows what responsibilities He's given us. He knows the circumstances He has allowed in our lives. He will help us adjust to meet that situation, but we always want to be coming back to a pattern whenever possible, because that is the way the mind works best.

Accomplish Your Purpose?

Another aspect of timing relates to the question of how much time. We've really answered this question when we've seen that meeting with God is a love friendship. The length of the time is inconsequential. If you're in love with someone, you don't count the minutes, except for the minutes you can't be with him or her. Yet, what is crucial is spending enough time to accomplish your purpose.

If I were engaged to be married and could only be with my mate five minutes a day, I wouldn't be accomplishing much toward building a deep friendship. So we need to be sure that the time we have is adequate enough to accomplish the goals and aims that we have for that time. Ten minutes a day is probably not sufficient to accomplish any meaningful goal. Twenty or thirty minutes is a minimum for getting our minds in a receptive gear, thinking through what we have gained, and then making it work in our lives.

There is one exception. If you are starting devotions for the first time, start with a minimum of ten minutes and build a habit; then stretch it to twenty or thirty as soon as possible. Simply give God all you've got. But strive for enough time to accomplish your goals for meeting with Him.

Never Misused—Only Multiplied

One other question often arises regarding the time we meet with God. We are often tempted to think that we don't have the time to spare. However, the opposite is really true, because it literally saves us time. Proverbs 10:27 says, "The fear of the Lord prolongs life." The Living Bible translates this same verse, "Reverence for God adds hours to each day." Experience bears this out. Martin Luther used to say that he had so much to do in a day that he couldn't afford not to spend at least four hours in prayer. He discovered the truth that time spent with God is never misused, only multiplied. This is true because God sharpens our minds, calms our fears, strengthens our memories, and enables us to do our work more efficiently. A person in tune with God will always be effective in his work. The inner peace that time with God gives enables us to do more quality work with more energy left over at the end of each day. In Acts 3:19 Peter told the Jews to "repent . . . and return . . . that times of refreshing may come from the presence of the Lord." Time spent with God always yields time for yourself. The more you give, the more you receive.

Balance vs. Habit

An important benefit of having a set time for God is that it helps to avoid the problem of habit. This may sound contradictory, but read on. Time with God does not always have to be fifty percent reading the Bible and fifty percent praying, or seventy-five percent this and twenty-five percent that. We're creatures of habit and we generally like things to be set and predictable. Now habits can be helpful, as we've mentioned, but they can also be hazardous. They can be harmful because we can begin to dig ruts so deep they keep us from becoming flexible with what the Spirit of God may be impressing upon us to do.

There may come a time when the Spirit of God says, "Study that passage a little longer, because there are some truths I really want you to learn." Or He may say, "Spend your whole time today studying the Scriptures. Forget about your praying; it's more important to Me that you understand this truth. I plan for you to use it soon." Or He may say, "There is someone I want to put on your heart. Don't just stop because it's ten minutes to seven. I want you to pray the whole time, because this person needs your prayers."

We need flexibility and willingness to bend our habits within the time we have set. If we find ourselves doing the same thing every day, we should try a change and be ready for an urging from the Spirit of God. Having a set time will help produce a sensitivity to the Spirit because of the consistency. A sporadic time will more easily lead to ruts, because we try to pick up where we left off and often find ourselves covering the same ground.

The Principle of Recording

The second powerful principle is *recording the results,* preserving the fruit of our efforts. Have you ever read a great passage of Scripture, found some new insights, and wanted to share them with your mate or a close friend? The next time you see them you start to share it, yet it doesn't quite come out as fresh as you remembered it. They politely say, "Oh, that's good," and you feel deflated.

Recording the results of our time with God is probably the most important thing we can do when we meet with Him. In the action we take, whatever our method or practice may be, remember this: The *measure* of a method is the *product* it produces. Recording the thoughts, the questions, or the principles we gain from our study is the fruit of our labor—fruit for our own enjoyment and for others.

What are we after when we meet with God? What is our goal—our aim? The best evaluation comes when we write down what we learn and feel. Let me suggest three reasons why recording what goes on as we meet with God is fruitful.

Write It or Lose It

First of all, our memory cannot retain everything we read. It cannot by itself organize a total picture of what we've just studied. It needs help. Retentive memory cannot become permanent without review and action. A record of the product of our study is the only basis for future use. A record preserves the findings and enables the mind to be free to move on to the next step or part of our study. If we try to hang on to a thought without writing it down, we will forget it every time. And don't be afraid to waste paper or fill up your Bible. I've got a lot of useless notes, but among those useless notes I have captured many significant truths from the Spirit of God.

Recording also gives you a picture of organized results. Give the mind loose data and it continually seeks to put it in some form or order. Take the order that your mind gains from your study or reading, and write it down. If you don't, it won't handle those isolated bits of information you gain. It will simply kick them out. Every thought has to have a framework and a place to fit or it will be lost forever.

Making It Your Own

The second reason for recording is that it permits us to see the course over which we've just traveled. This has the added value of enabling us to improve the plan we use. Many of us stagnate in our study because we don't improve what we're doing. Doing the same things over every day can cause us to lose interest. Recording enables us to review, examine, and evaluate our spiritual growth. This also helps us maintain consistency.

Moving the Hand Cements the Moment

A third reason why we should record is because we learn most thoroughly when we write. We learn best by doing. When we write our impressions, the action causes a deeper imprinting of the data on our brain, especially when we write in a significant way. For example, 2 Peter 1:5–7 records a list of progressive actions. Peter says, "For this very reason also, applying all diligence, in your faith supply moral excellence, and in your moral excellence, knowledge; and in your knowledge, self-control, and in your self-control, perseverance, and in your perseverance, godliness; and in your godliness, brotherly kindness, and in your brotherly kindness, Christian love." By writing these down as a list, we quickly understand that they are not isolated items. Each one of these ideas makes up a stair step. There is a definite progression that Peter has given in the Christian growth pattern, and they are interrelated. It was only by writing it down that I saw its significance. When the Scriptures give a list, record it as a list. Writing it out will give you new insights.

Charting Truth from the Bible

Another thing that can help significantly is using *creativity* in our recording. Charting the placement of the minor prophets, for example, can help you graphically identify when they prophesied, providing much greater significance to what they say. It wasn't until I figured out where they were in time sequence that I understood why they said what they did. Creativity helps clear up difficulties.

Comparing–Contrasting

Record your findings using comparisons and contrasts. Comparisons help highlight the similarities between things. Contrasts help us focus on the differences. Take a passage like Galatians 5. In it Paul contrasts the things that characterize the walk of the spirit and the things that mark the walk of the flesh. By listing those contrasts we can see just how important the differences are.

God Repeats Himself

Another helpful tool as you read God's Word is to record what is repeated—God's instant replay. When we read something more than once, that is always significant. Why? The Bible we hold in our hand is God's total Word to us. It can only contain so many words and, therefore, the Spirit of God was very economy-minded. He didn't waste words. Every word that is in it has a purpose. And anything that is given more than once has special significance. Therefore, whatever you see repeated, write it down and ask yourself, Why is God emphasizing that truth?

Recording Prayers

It is also helpful to record our prayers. I've written down some of my most important over the last ten years. As I look back through them, some of them have been answered with a "yes," and some with a "no," and some with a "wait." There are hundreds of prayer requests there. This practice helps me in several ways. As I go back over them, I am reminded of the great things that God has done for me. Even more important is what it has taught me about my praying.

I found that my earlier prayers were much too general. I would not have realized God's answers if my life depended on it. They were not stated well. Another thing I learned was that much of my praying was self-centered. The prayers only reflected my interests. Even though it was my prayer book, proportionately I was not including others as much as I try to now. Another error I saw was that often my prayers were stated in such a way that I wasn't praying according to Scripture. I wasn't really thinking clearly about the issue that was on my heart. I had written something down hastily without thinking it through. Recording my prayers helped me see all these things.

Finally, never depend on receiving a Spirit-given insight twice. The greatest memory is only as strong as the weakest ink. Remember the principles of *timing* and *recording the results* as you meet with God.

Write Your Own Psalm

Try writing a psalm in response to what you are experiencing and learning from God in your devotional time. It can be easy and very rewarding. My friend Glenn Plate suggested these five steps as a guide for writing your own psalm: (1) make a statement of praise, (2) write a brief introduction about your current situation—whether it be an experience of deep sadness or a feeling of joy, (3) reflect on your past or present need, (4) record the circumstances of your deliverance, and (5) renew your vow of praise and end with a statement of praise and honor to God, like the beginning. This is similar to the pattern used by the psalmists, so use it to assist you in your own expressions of praise and worship to God.

——— *Reflection* ———————————————
1. What is the real issue behind taking time with God when there is no time?
2. When is the best time for you to meet with God?
3. Most people experience guilt about time. What is your biggest struggle with it? How will you solve it?
4. How can recording your thoughts and insights help you?

CHAPTER TWELVE

Problems That Paralyze

Problems are God's megaphone to get your attention.
—C. S. Lewis

CLARENCE JONES HAD plowed around a large rock in one of his fields for years. He had broken several plowshares and a cultivator on it and had grown rather morbid about the rock.

After breaking another plowshare one fall, and remembering all the trouble the rock had caused him through the years, he finally determined to do something about it.

When he put his crowbar under the rock, he was surprised to discover that it was only six inches thick and that he could break it up easily. As he was carting it away he had to smile, remembering all the trouble that the rock had caused him and how easy it would have been to have fixed it sooner.

Take the Time to Fix It

There is a tendency in all of us to bypass small obstacles when we are in a hurry. We simply don't want to take the time to deal with them at the moment. Like the old farmer, we plow around it. Yet like that old rock, if it comes up over and over, we're much better off to take the time to fix it. We all have problems in our quiet times. Let's admit it and look for answers.

Four Giants

We found almost uniform agreement in the class. That was unique, especially for sixty-three men and women from all different backgrounds and generations. Out of all the problems of meeting with God, we agreed that there were four big ones. They seemed to loom like giants among all the other problems. These four seem to be universal.

There is *loss of concentration*. It likes to trap us in confusion and chain us to small accomplishments. There is *loss of feeling*. It likes to keep us guessing and take away our motivation. There is *lack of discipline*. It likes to keep us inconsistent and seldom on target. Finally, there is the biggest giant of all—*lack of practice*. It likes to keep our minds full, our hearts stirred, and our hands tied.

Giant No. 1—Loss of Concentration

The first giant in the land of our quiet time is loss of concentration. "How do I increase concentration and keep my mind from wandering?" The best way to answer this question is to ask it in another way. What are the causes of a lack of concentration?

Before you go any further, answer this question on a separate sheet of paper. What are four causes of concentration loss for you? Wandering thoughts, for example.

Grouping the Causes

Each of our lists will be expressed differently, but you probably guessed some of the following. To get a handle on them, let's group them this way.

There are *physical causes* for concentration loss. We get sleepy, hungry, cold or hot, sick, interrupted, or tired from a long day or short night.

There are *mental causes* for concentration loss. We get bored, reminded of other tasks, off on tangents, or we daydream.

There are *emotional causes* for concentration loss. We have guilt feelings, fears or anxieties, and anger.

Finally, there are *spiritual causes* for concentration loss. We fail to pray and fail to take seriously the fact that we are fighting a spiritual battle.

Any one of these can be sufficient to destroy concentration. So how do we handle them?

A Closet Climate—Physical Preparation

The physical causes for concentration loss can be met by physical preparation. We have to pick a time when we are least likely to be hungry or sleepy and pick a place where we will not be too hot or cold or interrupted.

If you have your quiet time in your bed, you are in a danger zone. Chances are ten to one you will go to sleep. I've done it a hundred times. If you are at home, take the phone off the hook or turn down the bell. Choose a room with a lock on it, so children cannot barge in. Remember Jesus Himself said go into your inner room and shut the door so you can pray in secret (Matthew 6:6).

The point is that if our quiet time is a true priority we must prepare for it as much as anything else. If you are sick or extremely tired, I believe God's Word to you is "go to bed and rest." Don't worry about lengthy prayers or Bible reading. We may feel that we have a spiritual problem, when actually we need a good night's sleep.

Cobweb Cleaning—Mental Preparation

Mental contributions to concentration loss likewise need mental preparation. Have you ever been bored with your Bible study? Have you ever jumped into an interesting book and a few minutes later found yourself wondering if you got everything ready for the fishing trip tomorrow, or if the oven was still on? Boredom and current events are regular killers of mental concentration.

Boredom or loss of interest is more common than we like to admit. A big reason for boredom is studying in the wrong place at the wrong time. Often we jump into a long book like Ezekiel and read about five chapters and find that our minds want to run everywhere but in Ezekiel. Why? Because we don't know anything about Ezekiel. We need some background. Get a study Bible or a one-volume commentary on the Bible and look for an overview. Many books of the Bible lose our interest because we get bogged down in the details of an ancient culture. But a little study and mental preparation can be profitable.

"The Good Idea" Problem

Probably the most frequent mental interrupter is the "good idea" or subconscious reminder of an important current event. When we think about the fishing trip or turning off the oven and it interrupts our concentration, what do we do? The greatest possible help is the use of a pad and pencil.

Many great ideas and sparks of creativity just pop into our minds at odd times. This is common to each of us. There is nothing sacred about our quiet time where these flashes of inspiration are concerned. Always keep a pad and pencil by your side when you have a few moments with God. Write down immediately every reminder or good idea that comes along. They could be from the Lord. They also may be legitimate responsibilities we should not forget. Writing it down only takes a few moments, but it will free your mind for longer moments of study. We don't have to worry that we will forget it. We *can* forget it for the time being *if* it is written down.

Say It When You Pray It

Another helpful suggestion for mental interruptions is praying out loud. Because our minds work so quickly it is easy for our minds to wander while we pray silently. If we pray out loud though, our minds are engaged in this conscious action and wandering thoughts are held back. So praying out loud is a big help in mental concentration.

Once visiting the Wailing Wall in Jerusalem, I noticed many of the Jewish men rocking back and forth as they prayed. I worked up the courage to ask one of them why they were rocking. He said, "We are commanded to love the Lord our God with all our heart, mind, soul, and body; and besides, it helps me to stay awake."

The Big Three—Emotional Preparation

A third cause for lost concentration is our emotions. Guilt, anger, and fear are the big three. If we are feeling one of these emotions, they will dominate our concentration until we deal with them. When we are not able to concentrate and can't trace it to a physical or mental cause, this is the best place to check. The emotions are closely related to the mental and spiritual areas. They frequently overlap. Begin to overcome emotional barriers by first checking for any unconfessed sin.

Unconfessed sin can cause all three of these emotions. We may feel guilt because we are guilty. We may feel anger because we've had a goal of some type that has been blocked. We may feel fearful because we lack faith in God's goodness and willingness to help.

Often sin comes from things we fail to do rather than something we actually did. Sin-caused emotions have the most clear-cut answer in the Bible. God will always cleanse and restore us if we confess—that means agree that it is sin and agree that it is forgiven (1 John 1:9).

Quiet Time Guilt

One other factor to remember is that some guilt is false guilt. Many of us have this deep suspicion that we haven't done all we should have done. We are covered over with "quiet time guilt." We haven't done it often enough, long enough, regular enough, or deep enough. Yet while this guilt is not always true guilt, it may be real if we have been negligent of our time with the Lord. If so we need to confess that. Remember, however, that the Lord never puts a limit or a time guide on our quiet times.

Emotion Control Button

The key to overcoming emotional disturbance is the satisfaction of obedience. Successful times with God are not measured by length or depth. They are measured in obedience. Obedience comes from two intertwined sources, a focus on the love of God and the help of the Holy Spirit. John says, "This is how we know that we love the children of God: by loving God and carrying out his commands" (1 John 5:2 NIV); and "we know that we live in him and he in us, because he has given us of his Spirit" (1 John 4:13 NIV). Love is the controlling emotion that helps concentration, and the Spirit enables us to keep love growing in our lives.

Forgetting the Real Battle

A final contribution to loss of concentration is found in the spiritual area. It is the most crucial because it is the most subtle. Paul himself said we forget so easily that our battles are not physical but spiritual (Ephesians 6).

We have a spiritual enemy. Jesus spoke of him and to him as a real person, a real foe. Paul said do not be ignorant of the Devil's schemes. He never attacks in the trivial, only in the crucial. He knows that a growing friendship with the Lord through regular meetings with Him is the most important target to hit. One of his greatest deceptions is to make us believe that God cannot be our closest friend nor should He be. He seeks to make us feel that God does not care about the things real friends do. This can make God appear like a distant relative with whom closeness is reserved only for special occasions. Satan does this by accusing and condemning us in our thought lives.

Consequently, we get conned into believing that those thoughts are from God. Naturally, this erects a barrier if it is not recognized. It can greatly affect our concentration.

Satan uses our minds to deceive us by planting many such thoughts. He may use anything to cause us to not see God as He really is. Our job is to stop this wrong thinking by the transforming of our minds. Paul says we can change our minds and thinking by bringing these wrong thoughts into captivity, by seeing them for what they really are—a deception. "But I am afraid, lest as the serpent deceived Eve by his craftiness, your minds should be led astray from the simplicity and purity of devotion to Christ" (2 Corinthians 11:3).

In the Middle of Everything

Have you ever been in a great mood on Sunday morning, enjoying the service, and in the middle of the pastor's prayer had a terrible thought flash through your mind? We want to blame ourselves; yet that thought, when not consciously brought on by our own efforts, can only come from one source—the Devil. At that moment we must pray and claim the Lord's power to remove it and return our attention to Him. We capture the thought and bring it into obedience as Paul explains (2 Corinthians 10:5). The best thing to do is pray along with the pastor, repeating his words in our minds; that locks our mind in the action of the moment.

Prayer is our most effective giant killer for all kinds of concentration breakers; then comes preparation, planning, and the pad and pencil. These tools can build an effective weapon to spring us from the trap of confusion and small accomplishments brought on by the confinements of concentration loss.

Giant No. 2—Loss of Feeling

The second giant that kills our time with God is loss of feeling. Do these statements sound as familiar to you as they do to me?

"Sometimes I just don't sense God's presence and I don't know why."

"When I have lost my love for the Lord, how do I make myself love Him again?"

"How do I worship when I really don't want to?"

"Is there something I can do about the down times in my spiritual life?"

We all tend to live by our feelings. "If it feels good, do it," we're told. Yet as Christians, our responsibility, according to the Bible, is to be in control of our feelings. We may not understand why we feel a certain way, but our emotions need to be under control. Emotions change rapidly due to the circumstances that we face, problems we encounter, and experiences we have. Feelings often come and go without our ever knowing why.

Talking to Yourself

The psalmist in Psalm 42:5 puts it so well. He realizes that his emotions are down, and he says, "Why are you in despair, O my soul?" He talks to himself. He says, Look, soul, why such hopelessness? Why have you become so disturbed? Here is a picture of a man whose will is in control of his emotions. He realizes his emotions are not measuring up to what he wants to experience, so he examines himself and asks himself, Why am I this way? The first thing to do is examine ourselves and ask the question, Why am I feeling this way? It may be an unconfessed sin, but then maybe it's something that we can't explain, something we have to trust God with.

The psalmist did the right thing by exhorting himself. He examined his emotions by asking himself, Why do I feel this way? And then he exhorted his emotions by saying, "Hope in God, for I shall again praise Him for the help of His presence" (v. 5). Count upon Him to reveal Himself to you. The last thing he did in verse 11 is remind himself, "Hope in God, for I shall yet praise Him, the help of my countenance, and my God." He said God is the one who helps our countenance—the outward expression of our inward condition. So examine yourself, exhort yourself, and remind yourself before God that He is the One who can help you deal with your feelings.

When the Feeling's Gone

When we lose our feelings for a devotional time, the most important thing for us to do is go on doing what we should be doing. Don't let your feelings be your guide. We might say, "I don't feel very good so I think I'll wait until my feelings change." We need to go on whether or not our feelings are positive. "Keep on trucking" is the answer to losing the feelings.

Change Them with . . .

The truth is, actions change feelings. Someone has said, "Act enthusiastic and you will be." Now, that is not just positive thinking. God doesn't want us to dismiss our feelings. We must learn, however, to acknowledge them and then express them in a way that honors God.

It is a lot easier to *act* ourselves into new *thinking* than it is to *think* ourselves into a new *action*. This means that if we don't have the right feelings, we shouldn't wait until they come. Just the opposite. We must work on our actions and the right feelings will follow.

I discovered this for myself when I wanted to have more personal worship in my devotional time. I began to take portions of the Psalms that contained worshipful phrases and say them to God as if they were my own words. It felt very awkward and unnatural at first. But the more I acted on my desire to worship Him, the more I began to enjoy it. Today I do it spontaneously every time I pray and it is one of the most enjoyable feelings and actions in my quiet time.

"I Do"

Sometimes I don't feel married, but I know I am. I have witnesses to the fact that I said, "I do," and she said, "I do." So the fact is, we are married whether I feel it or not. If the fact was only based on my feelings, I would have to get married again and again, because normal married life is as full of low days as high days. We cannot put our faith in our feelings. We can only put our faith in the facts. As I move on and act as though I am married, and do what I am supposed to do, that "married feeling" returns. It always does.

Every healthy relationship experiences ebb and flow. Our own emotions experience ebb and flow. The Lord understands when our friendship with Him is sometimes low on feeling. He allows our feelings to run low so we will remember that our love friendship with Him is not based on them, but on our commitment to Him.

When you have the spiritual "blahs" just go to the Lord and tell Him. He knows. Then go to the Psalms and read to see how many spiritual downers the psalmists had and what the writers did to rekindle their feelings.

When the Love Is Gone

Remember that it is possible to lose your love for the Lord. John reminds us in Revelation where Jesus tells the strong Ephesian church that the only thing He held against them was the loss of their first love. First love is that fresh sense of life in the friendship when we first fall in love. So we need to ask ourselves if we are getting stagnant in our feelings toward the Lord.

When prayer becomes dry, infrequent, or hard, think about someone you really admire or respect. Think about telling him why you appreciate him, then drop his name and insert God's. Tell Him all you admire and appreciate about Him. God is the one who made that person the way he is, so He holds all the same traits. In other words when feelings are dry, love what you can.

If you still feel "blah" check to see if there is any unconfessed sin. Make sure it is *unconfessed* sin, because the devil loves to remind us of old sins we've already confessed, but may still feel bad about. He can get you down even farther. If we are aware of sin, or through prayer the Lord reveals sin, that could be the reason for the "blahs." It may be that sin has caused anxiety or guilt, and one of those has crowded out our feelings of love and respect for the Lord. John reminds us that we are only a prayer away from renewed fellowship when we confess our sins (Revelation 2:5).

Balance

A friend once told me of a conversation he had with his son. The topic was the thirst for experience among today's young people. His son said, "Dad, the reason so many young people are turning to the Charismatic movement is because they want a way to express their feelings to God."

Why is this true? Many of our churches consider it improper for their members to openly express spontaneous joy and worship. Yet people want to express their feelings. And not just joy, but sadness as well. The key is finding an appropriate way.

There must be a balance.

Life brings all the feelings—some good, some bad. Larry Crabb, a clinical psychologist, says that emotional maturity is not the absence of negative feelings. We all feel anger, guilt, and fear. That is normal. An emotionally mature individual, however, is one who recognizes what the feelings are, admits them, and seeks to express them in the way that would best honor God.

Giant No. 3—Lack of Discipline

One of the toughest giants to deal with is lack of discipline. I know him well. He especially likes to torment me.

How do we discipline ourselves to be more consistent? Discipline is a problem of the will. It may be a matter of just plain laziness, but often mixed with laziness is a wrong view of faith. Some of us have a magical view of faith that implies that if I trust God everything will take care of itself—as if by magic. Just let go and let God. It is a subtle view that actually says, "We're not responsible for what happens; it's all under God's control."

This wrong view of faith is a big contributor to lack of discipline. In Philippians 2:13, Paul says, God "is at work in you, both to will and to work for His good pleasure." So God is at work in us; that's His part. Now hear what he has to say in the verse before: "Work out your salvation." That's our part. He is not saying that we work to get salvation, but the salvation we have we are to work out in our lives. The Christian life is God doing one hundred percent and our doing one hundred percent. We do it by faith in Him. We do all we can and He does what we cannot do. Some of us lack discipline because we are resting only on God's part. But He gives us responsibility as well.

Just Plain Lazy

A bigger cause of an undisciplined life is simple laziness. Laziness really needs to be called what it is—sin. God hasn't designed us to be lazy people, but our sin natures pull us in that direction.

When Adam fell, his nature was forever infected with sin. That diseased nature was passed on to us. Because of that, each of us has a problem with laziness in some area. We have an inherent tendency to be lazy—to *not* do the things of God.

It is a sin and it needs to be dealt with. I need to say, "Lord, I'm lazy, and I admit it. I have done this eighty-nine times this week, but I come before You to confess it and work at it again." Recognize laziness for what it is, and continue working to reestablish the right habits.

A Problem of Priority

The thorniest problem in discipline is that of keeping priorities. When we are not lazy and are properly viewing faith as our responsibility, but still struggle with discipline, the problem of priorities must be present. More people struggle with this than just about anything else. Remember again, the Devil is no fool. He wants to keep us bottled up. Encouraging fuzzy priorities or faulty priorities is his favorite trick.

When you think of priorities, ask three questions. The Scriptures give us the answers.

1. "What do I want in life?" This is the most important question we will ever ask. What do I want out of life? What do I want my time with God to be? What do I want my spiritual life to be like? What do I want to get out of it? What do I see in the Scriptures that I really want for my life? The kind of person we want to be must be clear in our minds. What we want our time with God to produce must be clear. We have to ask and answer that question. Do I really want to know God? Do I want to be a growing Christian? Do I want to express my love and worship to Him?

Do I want to be the kind of person who's obedient to Him? We must decide what kind of person we want to be.

2. The second question logically follows: "What is it going to take to get there?" What steps do I have to take? Will fifteen minutes, thirty minutes, or an hour a day get me there? Our strategy—meeting with God daily, or every other day, or three times a week—will determine whether or not we reach our goals. This is where we are dependent on the grace of God.

3. A clarifying question is, "How much am I willing to pay?" What is the price tag? It's going to cost something. What we invest to accomplish our goals will determine the quality of the product. This is by the help of the Holy Spirit and His leading.

It is not desire that changes a person's destiny; it is a faith-based decision. We've all got the desires. We all want to be like great Christian people we know and admire, but desire is not enough. We have to make a decision. I have to choose what I want in my Christian life—what kind of person I want to be. I've got to decide what I am willing to pay to get there. There is no shortcut to excellence. If we want excellent times with God, there will be a cost. Anything in life that is truly valuable has a high price tag. Christ paid the price, the Holy Spirit created the desire, yet we obey.

The Freedom of Discipline

You're only free when you're disciplined. For example, you have no freedom to play what you want on the piano until you've disciplined yourself to learn the basics. And you can only be free in the Christian life when you have disciplined yourself in the skill of Christian living.

This does not mean I am pulling myself up by the boot straps. God is so eagerly concerned about our having a holy and fruitful life that He works in us. The Living Bible paraphrases Philippians 2:13 this way, "For God is at work within you, helping you want to obey him, and then helping you do what he wants." God helps us by giving us the desire, then helps us fulfill our desires. He wants us to desire the discipline that we need to meet with Him. And He is willing to help us fulfill it, but we must act on those desires. Jerry Bridges, in his helpful book, *The Discipline of Grace*, said, "Our part is to work, but to do so in reliance upon God to enable us to work." God's work does not make our effort unneccessary, but rather makes it effective.

Motivation

Another very effective aid in overcoming our discipline problem is planning—a plan that clearly shows where we are going and what we are trying to accomplish. When time with God is drifting, often the problem is that we don't have any ultimate aim for that time. We need a plan. Plan your Bible study ahead of time. Decide on the length of time, number of chapters, and so on. Then sketch out what you want to pray before your prayer time.

The opposite of lack of discipline is motivation. Motivation is the shove that gets us out of the ditch, and it grows out of our discipline. One fruit of discipline is more motivation—like a generator. Motivation, however, is often stifled by our failure to plan. Once we decide what we want and what we are willing to pay, we can then begin to reach clear goals. As our discipline takes hold, our motivation will grow, which in turn will strengthen our discipline. Having a plan becomes the basis for this process.

Fifty Thousand Pounds of Profit

From Roaring Springs, Pennsylvania, this story came over the Associated Press wire service:

An estimated 2,000 persons from various parts of the U.S. gathered to honor a cow that set a world record for producing milk. Corine, a ten-year-old, 1,600 pound Holstein, totaled 50,759 pounds of milk over the last year. The average Holstein gives a little more than 13,000 pounds a year.

Kenneth Mallory, who shared the ownership of Corine, said, "She just has the will to milk." We have to decide whether or not we want to put out the average or produce our best. We can get 50,000 pounds of profit from meeting with God and His Word if we set our minds to doing so. It is no different from our homes or jobs. We can make it what we want it to be, by God's grace.

Habit Forming

Go for it and trust God. You may fail, but keep at it. It usually takes three months to set a habit in our lives.

If we decide, "I'm going to be more disciplined, and I'm going to meet with the Lord three times a week for thirty minutes," the first thing that usually happens is we wipe out. We blow it. We get all revved up and do it for two or three days; then the usual interruptions come along and the next thing we realize is that we haven't done it for a week. Usually out of guilt, we get back on it for three to four days and blow it again. At this point the Devil convinces most of us that we will never be disciplined enough and maybe we are not really ready for it right now. So we quit. This is the critical point where we need to keep after it more than ever. Don't focus on the failure, rather focus on Christ and the goal of a relationship with Him. Pick it up and do it again. If we keep at it for up to three months, meeting with God will become a habit.

The Devil's Favorite Tool

Once the Devil decided to go out of business, and he put all of his tools up for sale: bitterness, jealousy, strife, anger, hate. One of them, however, he wanted to keep. When asked what it was, he said, "Discouragement. It works so well on so many people in so many places." Unfortunately the Devil has not decided to go out of business, and discouragement is still a very real test for us all. Don't give up.

Permanent Changes

God doesn't worry about our momentary failures. He is far more concerned that we maintain obedience to Him. It has permanent effects. Psychological studies tell us that it takes at least three months for any effort to make a permanent change in a person's life. This is the "use it or lose it" principle. Remember, don't worry about failures. Keep working at it, and pretty soon it will become something that your mind will automatically remember.

The Bible is so full of admonitions and examples of discipline. One of my favorite examples is Ezra. Ezra 7:10 says, "Ezra had set his heart to study the law of the LORD, and to practice it, and to teach His statutes and ordinances in Israel." Ezra set his heart. He made a decision, a commitment. He would do whatever it took to study the law and to practice it. He decided what he wanted and how much he was willing to pay. Paul gives the same idea in 1 Timothy 4:7–8. He uses the example of the athlete: "Discipline yourself for the purpose of godliness, for bodily discipline is only of little profit, but godliness is profitable for all things, since it holds promise for the present life and also for the life to come."

Do I Have to . . .

One question comes up more than almost any other: "Do I have to have a quiet time every day?" The answer is a loud and clear, "No, you don't *have* to have it every day." Relief or shock? How can I be so definite? I can be definite in my answer because of what lies behind the question.

God tells us that our relationship with Him is like a marriage. As a married person, would I say to myself, "Do I have to meet with my mate every day to have a healthy growing relationship?" The answer is obviously no. But the real issue is why do I ask that question. A marriage partnership cannot be legislated; neither can a friendship be ordered.

Some people are surprised to discover that nowhere in the Bible are we told to spend time with God every day. We see examples, but we are never commanded to do it by God; that shouldn't be odd, because God wants to meet with us based on a motivation of love. If I am sick, on a business trip, or forced to work later than I had anticipated, have I lost my friendship with my wife? Of course not. This is the same with God. There are many times that my Bible study and prayer times get interrupted for urgent family and business matters and I have to change my schedule. I know my friendship with the Lord has not been altered one bit. I have certainly missed out on some blessings and enjoyment, but it hasn't changed His love for me or my love for Him.

This, of course, does not mean I haven't touched base. I call my wife when I'm going to be late or I am on a trip. And I certainly have those shorter calls to God on the telephone of prayer.

Therefore, my categorical answer of "no" to the question of a "*daily*" time" is based on the reason behind the question. Some of us have a rigid discipline out of fear or pride. Many of us feel that if we don't take the time, we will be out of God's will for the day or will sin as a result. This was the Pharisees' problem. They did not miss their scheduled time with God. But their hearts were not in it.

No Plateaus with God

Let's return to our analogy of marriage. If I continue to live a life that keeps me away from home on business for long periods, or my regular habit is to work long and late, or I let the day's priorities keep us apart, my marriage will ultimately fail. This is the same with God. We can lose touch with each other. We are either progressing in our friendship with the Lord or regressing. There is no middle ground. There are no spiritual plateaus in a friendship with God.

The more sporadic our meetings with God become, the less we desire to meet Him. The less consistent we are the less fruit we enjoy from the friendship.

He Waits to See Us

God is available every day. His presence does not depend on

physical closeness. We can leave our mates at home but we never leave the Lord. That is why we shouldn't see our meeting with God as a time or place or certain set of tasks. It is friendship. The psalmist says the Lord eagerly waits to see us each morning.

So if I ask the question, "Should I meet with God every day?" from this side of the coin the answer is yes.

"Do I have to?" No!

"Should I want to?" Yes.

When you feel that you "have to," it is probably better "not to." Instead, stop and ask why you feel that way.

If we see God as a friend, and the meeting time as time alone with Him and not simply a certain length of prayer or Bible study, then we will want to have it every day. We may not study our Bibles every day for an hour, but we may read it and think about it for ten minutes. We may not pray for thirty minutes every day, but we can pray several times for a few minutes throughout the day. The key is, Do you sense the friendship and respect and desire growing?

Different Needs

Just like any friendship, our friendship with God needs different things at different times.

A close friend, and a new Christian at the time, once asked me, "Should I spend more time in prayer or more time in Bible study?" I didn't really know how to answer him. I wanted to say they should be given equal time, but something wouldn't let me give such a pat answer. The real answer is, What you need the most at that time.

When our hearts are heavy with sorrow, or anxiety, or guilt, it is often best to spend a long time in prayer and get it all out before the Lord. We may have to take all the time we have that day, just to get our own emotions settled down. Are we out of fellowship if we ran out of time to read the Scriptures? No. We may have been in too bad a shape emotionally to have profited from the Word.

The next day we might sense the Lord's work in our lives and spend the whole time in the Word listening to Him. If we left no time to pray, does that mean we only had half of a quiet time? No! This is why we have to see meeting with God as flexible and personal. It is not rigid as to form, content, length of time, or frequency.

To Be the Greatest

We must end our discussion of discipline and daily time with God on this note: the more consistent it is, the better. The more often it is, the better. The longer it is, the better. Just like any important relationship, the better the consistency, frequency, and length I commit to it, the greater it will be.

Therefore, again we must ask, "What do we want in our Christian life?" Our goal is to strive to have longer more frequent times with the Lord. He wants us to give Him the most and the best we can in the friendship because He loves us. He wants to be with us. Our highest motivation can only be His love for us. This is what motivated David to say in the first psalm—happy is the one who delights in the law of the Lord and meditates on it day and night. The more time we spend with the Lord, the more we want to because of His love for us. David had it daily to some extent, if only a prayer before bed, but evidently it was on his mind throughout each day (Psalms 25:4–5; 63:6; 119:55, 97).

Giant No. 4—Lack of Practice

The Goliath of time-with-God killers is lack of practice. He is really the smartest and most powerful of the giants. He does not stop the quiet time; he stifles it. He does not crash the quiet time; he simply contains it.

Once we understand time with God as an expression of a love friendship, we understand how crucial practice is. Real love means action. Love is not only the expression of endearing words to one another; it is the expression of endearing work to one another.

This is why Jesus expressed His love to Peter by seeking him out when Peter felt all was lost. After denying his Lord, he went back to the only thing he knew—fishing. Jesus came after him and forgave him in a most wonderful way. Peter had denied the Lord three times, so Jesus asked Peter three times if he loved Him. The Lord enabled Peter, for Peter's sake, to reaffirm his love.

In the very act of reaffirming their relationship, the Lord taught Peter something about love. He said, "Peter do you love me? tend my lambs;" "Peter, do you love me? shepherd my sheep;" "Peter, do you love me? tend my sheep." The point He was making was this—Peter, if you really love Me, show Me; show yourself by doing My work. We only really love someone when we love him the way he wants to be loved. Jesus wants us to love Him by loving those He loves; that's doing His will.

Wasting Work

If we never aim to practice God's Word as a result of our meeting time, then the value of the meeting has been determined. All time with God should lead to worship and service. Practice becomes a significant consequence of our time with God. It is no wonder that our spiritual arch enemy sends a Goliath to kill this part of our meeting. If it can be contained, stifled, or simply diluted, the enemy has won.

It is a well-known fact that most Christians are not regular Bible readers. Fewer still actually study their Bibles regularly. And an even smaller percentage seek to consistently practice God's Word. Why? Many never get to first base because of the first three giants. Rounding third base is where practice begins, and somewhere between first and third looms this killer—lack of practice!

New Changes Daily? No!

Let's examine practice. What are we after? Should we expect to discover and apply some new truth every time we meet with God? I don't think so. Talking with Bible teachers, I've learned that it's not really workable to make a definite, clear-cut action plan every day. For example, if I study in Ephesians one day and come up with an action to take, something I'm going to definitely do, and then the next day I come up with another action plan, and the next day another, I will end up either with a long list of small things to do or a long list of major changes to make. I may not physically be able to do them all. It depends on what they are. If I decide God is telling me to change my lifestyle, slow it down, I can't do that in one day's time. God may instead tell me the same thing every day for several weeks because it is a big change to make and it will take time. Or He may remind us of one small thing to do this week and nothing else for several days.

The way the Holy Spirit seems to work is more along the lines of bigger areas in our lives. I don't find Him normally giving me an item or more a day. It would be impossible to make that many changes in my life. The deep changes that occur in our lives are the changes that occur over a period of time—the things we think deeply about and struggle with. Scripture does not indicate that a new or different application should be made every day. The Spirit of God is at work in my life to do God's will daily, but I find I'm doing well to absorb and practice one new truth every few weeks. These deeper changes come from things that we keep thinking about and working out in our lives over the long haul.

New Deeds Daily? Yes!

Let's further clarify this issue of daily practice. One thing that helps is to make the distinction between applying God's Word to my life—changing destructive habits, breaking wrong thought patterns, conquering a stubborn sin—and doing God's Word for others. In that sense we could gain a new application every day. We want to look for these daily—good deeds, kind words, spontaneous prayers.

If we examine ourselves closely, we don't find God giving a new word every day for big changes. As we grow in Christ and become more familiar with His Word, we already know what to do on a daily basis. The Lord expects us to do those things

with fewer reminders. What He does have to continually remind us of is to keep our lives clean and keep changing for
Him. This is where practice takes a slower turn. God is more
interested first in a quality of life than a quantity of good deeds.
It is too easy to do good deeds in our own energy without a
pure life to back it up.

God's Gaps

It never ceases to amaze me, when digging into the Old Testament characters, to find that God dealt with them over very
long periods of time. The records indicate there were long gaps
between God's conversations with Abraham. He would tell
Abraham to do something, then not speak again for months,
even years. God was giving Abraham time to live out His promises, to live by faith. It was a test for Abraham.

It was the same for Moses, David, the prophets, and even
Paul. After Paul first came to know Christ as Savior, a gap of
several years followed before he returned to the scene. The
Lord simply took His time to prepare Paul for all that he was
to do.

The point is that our ways and thoughts are not God's ways
and thoughts. His ways and thoughts are higher than ours (Isaiah
55:6–11). His Word is like a seed; it does not return empty, it
yields fruit; but it takes time for that fruit to come.

Practice is a process and not merely a one-time act. We learn
to keep doing God's Word and continue its work over the long
haul. This is what makes the permanent changes in our lives
and others'.

A Starting Gun

What can help us draw clearer insights to the practice of
God's Word? We need to ask ourselves some important questions before we make a plan of action. Because the Christian
life is really a series of relationships, to faithfully apply His
Word we need to ask some questions about those relationships.

───── *Reflection* ──────────────────

1. When does loss of concentration hit you most? What do you do about it?
2. How do you handle the loss of positive feelings?
3. What is your biggest discipline problem? How do you plan to overcome it?
4. What is the relationship between big changes and small deeds in our daily practice of meeting with God?

CHAPTER THIRTEEN

Quiet Time Application

We do not become more holy either by discipline or dependence. Neither do we become more holy by committing ourselves to God, or by developing Bible-based convictions. We become more holy by obedience to the Word of God, by choosing to obey His will as revealed in the Scriptures in all the various circumstances of our lives.
—Jerry Bridges, *The Discipline of Grace*

MAKING APPLICATIONS FROM your Bible reading or study is more effective when it is applied to relationships.

Take the truth you have learned and ask, How does this affect . . .

My perceptions of myself?
- My past background and heritage
- My present experience
- My personal values, priorities, standards
- My future expectations

My relationship with God?
- A command to obey
- Fellowship to enjoy

- Promises to claim
- Prayers to express

My relationships with others?
- In my home
- In my church
- In my social life
- In the world
- In my business (work)

My relationship with the Enemy?
- A person to resist
- Devices to recognize
- Sins to avoid
- Armor to wear

(Adapted from Irving L. Jensen's *Enjoy Your Bible*)

Asking the Right Questions

To get the most out of your Bible reading or study, start by asking questions that emphasize the key relationships in your life. Ask yourself, first of all, How does this truth relate to me? How does this truth affect my heartache? What area in my life really needs work in light of what I've just read?

Then consider what it says about God. How does this affect my friendship with Him? What is this idea telling me to do for God? Is there a promise I can apply? What have I learned about Christ?

A third question to ask is, How does this concern others around me? My family, friends in my church, the non-Christians that live and work around me—in what way do these truths affect them?

Next ask, Does this concern the enemy? We have mentioned how the enemy often seeks to hinder our concentration, play with our feelings, and tempt us. So ask yourself, Is God reminding me of the enemy? Because he's a person to resist, is God reminding me to resist Satan? Has Satan been tempting me with a sin I need to avoid? Satan has several schemes that we need to recognize (2 Corinthians 2:11; 11:3, 14).

The Generalities Game

Practice by asking these questions and writing out the answers as clearly and fully as possible. Next write out a planned action. It is at this point that another practice killer comes into play—generalities. If we get the area of work pin-pointed we've rounded second base, but to get past third we've got to get specific.

Most of the time, practice is not specific. The plan of action is not spelled out in detail. A great help is this four-line phrase:

Knowing this truth _____ (*the one you want to apply*)
I desire to _____ (*the action*)
by _____ (*means or plan*)
on this day(s)_____ (*choose a day on your calendar*)

For example, after reading about praying for each other, we may decide that we have neglected to pray sufficiently for our mates or parents or a certain friend. We can then fill in the lines like this:

Knowing this truth *about prayer* _____
I desire to *pray more for my wife* _____
by *praying three times weekly before I go to work* _____
on this day(s) *Mon., Wed., and Fri. at 7 a.m.* _____

We fail to get specific because we don't nail down *what* we are going to do, *how* we are going to do it, and *when* we are going to do it.

The Action Is the Proof

A short moment of personal evaluation by God's Word is worth more than hours of exposure to Bible lectures. Unless the Word is evaluating our lives, it is missing its purpose (Hebrews 4:12). A specific action is the final test of meeting with God. Jesus said, "Why do you call Me, 'Lord, Lord,' and do not do what I say? Everyone who comes to Me, and hears My words, and acts upon them, . . . he is like a man building a house, who dug deep and laid a foundation upon the rock" (Luke 6:46–48).

The late President Dwight Eisenhower, speaking at the National Press Club, once told his audience that he regretted he was not more of an orator. "It reminds me of my boyhood days on a Kansas farm," he said. "An old farmer had a cow that we wanted to buy. We went over to visit him and asked about the cow's pedigree. The old farmer didn't know what pedigree meant, so we asked him about the cow's butterfat production. He told us that he hadn't any idea. Finally, we asked him if he knew how many pounds of milk the cow produced each year. The farmer shook his head and said: 'I don't know. But she's an honest old cow and she'll give you all the milk she has!' Well," Ike concluded, "I'm like the cow: I'll give you everything I have."

Let's give God all we have when we meet with Him. That's action that builds upon a rock—remembering that I continually need to call upon His grace and the power of the gospel to enable me to persevere for His glory.

───── *Reflection* ────────────────────────

1. How can you best use these application suggestions?
2. What is the first thing you can do to act on these principles?

CHAPTER FOURTEEN

Meeting with God

We mutter, we sputter, we fume and we spurt, we mumble and grumble, our feelings get hurt. We can't understand things, our vision gets dim, when all that we need is a moment with Him.

—Corrie ten Boom

TODAY HE IS A MILLIONAIRE, but in 1932 Charles Darrow was broke and out of a job. And his wife was expecting a baby. He was trained as a heating engineer, but no jobs were available. Darrow and his wife just barely got by on the few odd jobs he could find as a handyman. Things were bleak.

But Charles and his wife were happy together. To take their minds off of their troubles and to fill their time, they made up a little game and pretended to be millionaires. Recalling pleasant vacations in Atlantic City, they made up a game with a boardwalk, and carved hotels and houses out of wood. In 1935 they marketed the game through Parker Brothers and literally became millionaires. The game—*Monopoly*.

They benefited from recalling happy times with others. That is exactly what God wants for us as we meet with Him—to enjoy the boardwalks of life even when they bring pain. We will benefit from our time with Him—enough to be spiritual millionaires.

Each meeting with God is different just as each of our walks with Him is different.

Think about it; only two men ever made it to heaven alive—Elijah and Enoch. They were as different as night and day. Elijah was carried away in a chariot of fire. His life was filled with miracles and mysteries. He called down fire from heaven, divided rivers, prayed up a drought, prayed down a storm.

In contrast Enoch walked quietly with the Lord for over three hundred years but was also taken up to heaven by the Lord. As one little girl put it, "Enoch went out on a walk with God and walked so far that when it got dark God said, 'Enoch, just come on home with me.' "

It seems, with these two extremes, that all the rest of the biblical characters fall in between. Here they are in all their splendor.

Adam blew it over a piece of fruit.

Noah built his ark and got drunk.

Abraham's fiasco with Hagar and Ishmael formed the basis of today's Israeli-Arab conflict.

Moses couldn't keep his cool and got left out of the Promised Land.

Miriam got jealous of her brother.

David had a problem with sex.

Job became self-righteous.

Solomon couldn't handle his wives.

Jeremiah wished he had never been born.

Jonah tried to run away from God.

Peter tried to keep Jesus from the cross.

Paul and Barnabas argued so heatedly they had to part ways.

Timothy was insecure.

Sound familiar? Did all these folks have perfect Bible studies and prayer lives? Of course not! But they learned to walk with their Lord. They learned to love Him. They knew He was really there every day—that He cared about everything that happened to them. And even in the midst of all their imperfections and failures, He loved them deeply.

Whether your life is fiery and filled with miracles like Elijah, or very quiet and routine like Enoch, or filled with many of the heartaches and problems that our friends in the Bible experienced, God is for you.

He is a day-by-day friend and the mighty God, all at the same time. He is mysterious and unfathomable, yet clear and easily understood. He is high and lifted up, yet merciful and full of grace. He is to be feared and obeyed, yet is intimate and patient. Best of all, He is knowable and lovable.

John said, "And we know that the Son of God has come, and has given us understanding, in order that we might know Him who is true. . . . We love, because He first loved us" (1 John 5:20, 4:19).

What is the measure of meeting with God? How do I know my moments with Him are meaningful and valuable?

The answer—Is He my Friend? Am I growing in my knowledge of Him? Can I fail, feel miserable, but still find that He loves me and accepts me? Am I discovering a little more of His power in my life as I take small steps of faith?

I still struggle with consistent Bible study and deep prayer. I don't know anyone who doesn't. That is what makes me know I'm on the right track. Can you ever get enough of a good thing—how about a good God? He pours out His love, His patience, His forgiveness—He has a purpose and plan for our lives. We matter to Him.

That makes it hard to skip out on meeting with Him.

God is eager to meet with you—for any length of time (Psalm 139:17–18). His loyalty and love will keep your heart focused on Him. Give yourself to Him and find all that He has for you!

Jeff Wells wanted to give his all for God. He ran in the 1978 Boston Marathon. At the halfway mark he said he felt too good and began to kick it. Toward the end Bill Rogers, who was always the man to beat, was ahead but Jeff was only one hundred yards behind with a long mile to go. At the very end of the race Jeff was only three seconds behind Rogers and closing fast. A police motorcycle suddenly closed in behind Rogers and

Jeff had to run around it to keep from falling down. If he had had twenty more yards, he would have beaten Rogers.

When asked how he felt after the race, Jeff said, "Too good. I told the Lord I wanted to do my best for Him, but I had too much left over at the end."

Let's give our all to God—to know Him, to be with Him—and not have to say when it is all over—I had too much left over to give.

—— *Reflection* ——————————————

1. Are you satisfied with what you give to God in your own quiet time?
2. Are your moments with God meaningful and valuable?

PART THREE

A Quiet Time "How-To"

CHAPTER FIFTEEN

A Picture of Worship

TIME WITH GOD IS IMPORTANT—we are told—but we are often not sure what it really is. It so easily can become a ritual that we crank out—one that often can feel horribly impersonal.

However, we have found that it begins with a personal God who wants us to know Him—who wants an intimate friendship—who wants our love. We have found that the aim of this time with God is first toward Him and not toward ourselves. However, we have also discovered that if we seek to express our love toward God and obey Him, our needs, hurts, and problems get met in the process. There is no giving without receiving in return.

So, this time with God we call devotions or quiet time or Bible study is where we seek to have the deepest of friendships with God. It is true that He is Lord and we are but servants—but He has seen to it that we are much more. He has made us a part of His family and has thus reserved for us the best of true friendship—love, admiration, respect, loyalty.

Our time with Him then shows our commitment to Him, by obeying and worshiping Him. This is the highest expression of our friendship. God seeks our worship—private as well as public.

At this point we readily remember that it is still so easy for the quiet time to not have all we've said above. God can seem very distant and impersonal. To deepen this sense of knowing God and loving Him, and to regain that personal part to meeting with God, let's go back to the beginning and see how God started it.

God gave Israel their rituals and prescribed them in certain ways for a reason. They were visual aids to help the Israelites know what God was like. They were given to help them know that God—though He was holy, righteous, and almighty—was also forgiving, approachable, and desirous of fellowship with them. He wanted them to have a personal relationship with Him.

The problem arose when Israel forgot the reason for their rituals. They lost the personal when they began to look at themselves rather than God. They began to disobey God and do what was right in their own eyes.

We are no different. Whenever we try to use God for our own purposes or ignore Him, the personal side of the relationship stops. The answer to keeping it personal is found in true worship.

The How-To

Has God given us any clues to worship? Yes, and they come from what He has said about public worship in the Old Testament. Our public lives should not be any different from our private lives.

In the Old Testament, people came to the tabernacle or temple to worship, but in the New Testament we find that the God of the tabernacle and temple has come to dwell in us. We have become "personal temples" so to speak, personal places of worship (2 Corinthians 6:16).

What is involved? The Old Testament worship at the tabernacle seemed rather elaborate and complicated. Is there an easier way to put this thing into practice and keep it all together? Yes, something that has already proven to be of tremendous help to many is to use the tabernacle as a prayer guide. Please note, however, that this is not meant to be the *only* way we should worship God.

Worship is expressed most deeply through prayer—the simple

enjoyment, love, and conversation with God. When I use the term *prayer guide*, I am including worship. Prayer has several elements, and worship is one of them. Let's look at an overview of the parts and then take each one separately.

Aid to Understanding

This overview is a mental picture to help us understand worship and to put the different aspects of prayer together. All memory experts tell us the best way to remember something is to put the idea into a picture in our mind. This is what we will be able to do with the tabernacle as a prayer guide.

The idea comes from Exodus 25:8–9. God, talking to Moses about the tabernacle, said, "Let them construct a sanctuary for Me, that I may dwell among them" (v. 8). God wanted to come down and be with His people. "According to all that I am going to show you, as the pattern of the tabernacle and the pattern of all its furniture, just so you shall construct it" (v. 9). God said, "There's something I want to you to see, and I want you to get the picture. Build a tabernacle just exactly as I show you."

God gave Moses a glimpse of something which gave him a picture of the tabernacle that he built. By God's design, the New Testament writer of Hebrews picks up on this idea in chapter 8. The book of Hebrews shows the fulfillment of many of the Old Testament symbols in the person of Jesus Christ. He discusses the priests and the sanctuary and says that the priests serve as copy and shadow of the heavenly things—the same things Moses was told by God when he was about to erect the tabernacle. God said to make all things according to the pattern which He showed Moses on the mountain.

God said the same thing to David when he was preparing the temple for Solomon to build. In 1 Chronicles 28:19 David says, "All this the Lord made me understand in writing by His hand upon me, all the details of this pattern." David is telling us that God gave him every detail of the temple. Why? God must have wanted the way He was worshiped and approached to be a certain way. The temple layout was essentially the same as the tabernacle, only more elaborate.

God showed Moses a view of heaven, and in effect said to Moses, "I want you to lay out the worship on earth just like it is in heaven." The tabernacle was going to be an illustration of worship for His people so that God could come and dwell among them and they could come to a Holy God and worship Him. They were to be a nation of priests and were to be an example to the whole world, so we could know how to come to God. The Lord wanted David to carry over the same truth and picture many years later.

What is this picture that the tabernacle and temple show us about worship? Let's use the simpler tabernacle as our guide.

The Tabernacle—Forgotten Symbol

The tabernacle had a cloth curtain that went all the way around it. It was folded up in the middle on the east side for the gates. Entering the courtyard there were two pieces of furniture, the brazen altar for burnt offerings called the altar of sacrifice, and then a smaller object in the middle which was the laver, where the priests washed their hands. The priests could then go through the curtains of the tent into the Holy Place, and the Holy Place held three pieces of furniture. There was the candlestick or the lampstand, the altar of incense, and the table of shewbread. Behind the altar of incense was a very thick veil which divided the Holy Place from the Holy of Holies. In the Holy of Holies the actual presence of God dwelt. Not that He wasn't anywhere else at the same time. But it was there where God's visible expression of Himself dwelt for the people of Israel at that time.

Be Careful

The Israelites had this elaborate system of worship as a reminder to them that their God was Holy and above all other gods. A person didn't just put up an altar anywhere. He had to realize that God was holy and righteous. This is symbolic for us

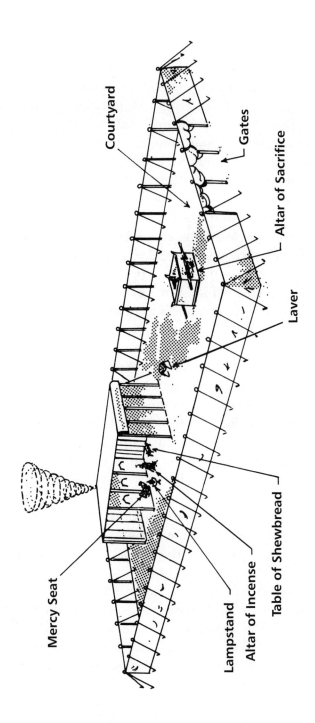

Tabernacle

in that we must have a proper attitude about our approach to God in prayer.

Solomon has beautifully stated this in the book of Ecclesiastes. He says, "Guard your steps as you go to the house of God, and draw near to listen rather than to offer the sacrifice of fools; for they do not know they are doing evil" (5:1).

Solomon saw that people who came and just babbled on before God, without considering what they were doing, did not have the right attitude before Him. Then Solomon adds, "Do not be hasty in word or impulsive in thought to bring up a matter in the presence of God. For God is in heaven and you are on the earth; therefore, let your words be few" (5:2). Solomon is telling us that when we come before God in prayer and talk with Him, we must come with an attitude of reverence and realize who we are coming before. Don't be hasty. Remember, it is like friendship, and we can't hurry a friendship.

In *Pilgrim's Progress* John Bunyan wrote, "In prayer, it is better to have a heart without words than words without heart." He is saying we must have a right heart attitude. We need to be right before we come to God. We cannot come before Him flippantly and say, "God, You have to do this for me—You've got to get me out of this." I am not saying that to be heard we have to be precise in every prayer, or that we cannot bring urgent things before Him, but we need to be careful that we don't come de-manding things from our great God in Heaven. Come, instead, with respect and love. Our normal prayers are not to be hurried, but given with the right spirit and attitude before Him. He is a person (a very special person) and not a vending machine.

The tabernacle helps us see what this special friendship with God requires. Remember that the common Israelite never got beyond the outer court area. They could come in to the court-yard through the gates, but only the priests could go in to the Holy Place, and only the high priest could enter the Holy of Holies. It is special for us to understand what Peter tells us in 1 Peter—we are a priesthood! We are called priests to God, so we all can have direct access to God.

Let's look at the separate parts and see how uniquely they act as a prayer guide.

Entering into Prayer

The first things we would see at the tabernacle are the *gates.* Psalm 100 provides a clue to their importance. Verse 4 says, "Enter His gates with thanksgiving, and His courts with praise." The Hebrews had a certain way of coming before God.

Worship began when the worshiper went to the gates to give thanks. They were to have thanksgiving in their hearts toward God. Psalm 92:1–2 says, "It is good to give thanks to the LORD, and to sing praises to Thy name, O Most High; to declare Thy lovingkindness in the morning."

So approaching the gates, we would be reminded of the privilege of coming to God each day. It was a place to give thanksgiving to Him. Paul makes reference to this in the New Testament. In 1 Thessalonians 5:18, he says, "In everything give thanks; for this is God's will for you in Christ Jesus." No matter what happens to us, God wants us to first give thanks to Him (Philippians 4:6). Giving thanks sets the tone as we come to Him. If we honestly give thanks, even when we may honestly be saying to God, "It's really hard to give thanks today," our perspective will be affected. Paul tells us in Romans 1:21 that an unthankful person is in sin. He says that those who have turned from God do not honor Him or give thanks to Him.

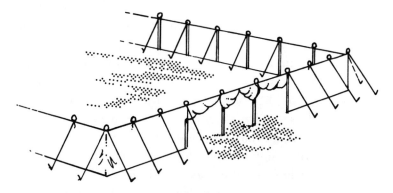

Gates and Courtyard

John tells us in Revelation 4, 7, and 11 that thanksgiving is constantly being offered to God by the angels, the elders, and other beings in heaven. In 1 Corinthians 1:4, Paul implies that we should give thanks constantly. He does not mean that you walk around, saying, "Thank You, thank You, thank You," but that in the course of our daily activities, we say, "Thank You, Lord, for the opportunities that You've given today. Thank You for getting us here safely. Thank You for this time to study Your Word and think about You." Or, "Thank You, Lord, for this trouble, this ache—not because it is good, but because You are good and You promise to work it out for good as I trust You" (Romans 8:28).

Surprise in a Traffic Jam

One morning the traffic was especially heavy. The cars looked like ants pouring out of ant hills that had been stepped on. I was late, and every route was backed up. I could not get to school. How was I going to be thankful for this? I said the words, only half meaning them. I was almost to school when I saw a hitchhiker. I don't pick up hitchhikers usually, but what could I do when traffic was inching along and a young man looks right at you with his thumb out? He could have walked faster than I was going. Okay, I'll pick you up, I said uncomfortably to myself. So I stopped and he got in the car and started talking. I was feeling rather bold, perhaps because he had interrupted my solitude. I began to tell him a little about myself and how I hadn't found any meaning in life until I met God in a personal way.

The next thing I knew he said, "I really want to know about God." If I had stayed angry with the traffic and let it control my attitude, I might not have picked him up. Only afterward could I really say, "Thank You for delaying me." God had a reason and worked what I considered bad into good. We don't always find out why, but He does have His reasons. Giving thanks, even when you don't feel like it, can help.

So as we look at the tabernacle as a guide for our prayer life, our first approach in prayer is thanksgiving. It's the first thing that I do in my own prayer life. It sets the attitude. As we come before God in prayer, we might say, "Lord, thank You so much for choosing me to love. Thank You for making me a part of Your family. Thank You for my wife and children. Thank You, Lord, for the good health that we've had this year. Thank You, Father, for friends, for Your provision for my needs. Thank You, Lord, for all these things." You can't help beginning to have a good attitude when you start thinking about all that God has done for you.

Giving Praise

The remaining half of Psalm 100:4 says, "And [we enter] His courts with praise." Is there a difference between thanksgiving and praise? Yes. Thanksgiving focuses on what God has done for us and praise focuses on who God is. If I tell my wife that she is a wonderful person because she cooks my meals, that is a good thing to do. If, however, I tell her she is wonderful because she is kind, loving, friendly, and fun to be with, I have said something entirely different. Praise is your appreciation of a person's worth. We have come a step closer to worship. The word *worship*, remember, comes from the word *worthiness*. We express the worthiness of a person when we praise him.

C. S. Lewis, in his book *Reflections On The Psalms*, says he had a hard time with the thought that we are supposed to praise God, especially the notion that God demanded it. He knew that God didn't need our praise, but he didn't understand why He asked for it.

The most obvious fact about praise—whether God or anything—strangely escaped me. I thought of it in terms of compliment, approval, or the giving of honor. I had never noticed that all enjoyment spontaneously over-flows into praise. The world rings with praise—lovers praising their mistresses, readers praising their favorite poet, walkers praising the countryside, players praising their favorite game. I had not noticed how the humblest, and at the same time most balanced and capacious minds, praised most, while cranks, misfits, and malcontents praised least. I had not noticed, either, that just as men spontaneously praise whatever they value, so they spontaneously urge us to join them in praising it: "Isn't she lovely? Wasn't it glorious? Don't you think that magnificent?" The Psalmists, in telling everyone to praise God, are doing what all men do when they speak of what they care about. I think we delight to praise what we enjoy because the praise not merely expresses, but completes the enjoyment. It is not out of compliment that lovers keep on telling one another how beautiful they are; their delight is incomplete till it is expressed! Fully to enjoy is to glorify. In commanding us to glorify Him, God is inviting us to enjoy Him.

Once inside the tabernacle, the first piece of furniture you would see would be the large *altar of sacrifice*. It was a big bronze structure with horns on each corner. It evoked a mixed sense of fear and relief. Here your animals died for you. God wanted the Israelites to realize that they could not come any closer to God without a sacrifice for their sins. Dealing with sin was of crucial importance.

To New Testament believers, this altar represents Jesus Christ's death for our sins. Unless there is a sacrifice, we can go no farther. Acceptance of Christ as the One who sacrificed for sinners is the realization of what it means to be a Christian. Here we remind ourselves of that fact.

Altar of Sacrifice

Me? A Sacrifice?

Now when we carry that thought into the New Testament and look for the idea of sacrifice as it relates to us, we would be easily drawn to Romans 12:1. "I urge you therefore, brethren, by the mercies of God, to present your bodies a living and holy sacrifice, acceptable to God, which is your spiritual service of worship." Not only is Jesus Christ a sacrifice for me, but He desires me to give my life as a sacrifice for Him. What does that mean?

In the Old Testament, animals placed on the altar were cut in pieces. The different parts of the animals meant different things. Each part was symbolic (Leviticus 1–7).

If I'm to be a living sacrifice, what are the parts I can offer to Him? Think of it in this way.

Lord, take my *hands* and use my hands today to show love, to shake Jack's hand and mean it, to put my arm around Bill and show him that I care, to do Your work today.

Take my *feet* and go where You want to go, through me. With them go over to the hospital and visit Jan, through me. Let me be faithful to go and be what You want me to be.

Take my *eyes* and help me see Beth as You see Beth. See through me today. Let my prayer be, "Lord, help me to have compassion; help me to see others as You see them."

Take my *mouth*, and help me to offer praise and thanksgiving, to say something that will encourage June; because so many times I say something that tears her down. I may think I'm only joking, but it might hurt her. Help me not to be a gossip, but use my mouth to encourage and build up. Help me to make Terry feel important today.

Use my *mind* to think Your thoughts. Help me to bring every thought into captivity, into the obedience of Christ (2 Corinthians 10). When I find a jealous thought coming into my mind, remind me to grab that thought and say, "Lord, help me bring that into control."

These are the things that I remind myself as I walk through the tabernacle and come to the altar of sacrifice. Jesus is a

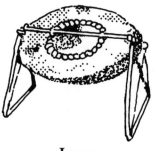

Laver

sacrifice for me and yet this is what it means for me to be a sacrifice for Him.

The next object you would come to is the *laver*, or bowl, where the priests washed before entering the Holy Place. The laver was a highly polished bowl made of the hand mirrors the women of Israel had offered. It was filled with clear fresh water. It was directly behind the altar of sacrifice and in front of the door to the Holy Place. The glistening water was a reminder to seek cleansing—proceed no further without being made clean.

The laver reminds us that Jesus Christ has washed away our sins, once for all. When we come to meet with Him, we must deal with our specific sins at that time.

At this point, we ask the Holy Spirit to help us remember any sin in our lives. It is the work of the Holy Spirit to convict us of sin. When we respond properly to the work of the Holy Spirit's convicting, we are to confess the sins we are reminded of. First John 1:9 says that Jesus "is faithful and just to forgive us our sins and to cleanse us from all unrighteousness (1 John 1:9 NKJV). So we ask the Holy Spirit to bring to mind any sin. They usually come pretty quickly.

A Warning—Old Sins

Don't dwell too long on confession. Satan loves to remind us of some of the old sins and the guilt we have felt in the past. We can very soon find ourselves confessing how bad we were and confessing sins we have already confessed. When this happens, Jesus is standing in heaven saying, "What are you talking about? I told you that I took those sins and separated them from you as far as the east is from the west. I threw them into the deepest sea. Don't you see the 'no fishing' sign? I've already dealt with those sins." So we must be careful not to get too introspective about our lives at that point.

It is good several times a year to take a thorough inventory of your life and think through what you're doing, where you're going, your motives, your thoughts. But don't do this on a day to day basis. Remember, it's the Spirit's job to convict us of sin. He works on our conscience. We ask Him to bring sin to mind and if nothing comes to mind, then in faith we can say, "Lord, thank You that You've dealt with my sins. If there is some sin of omission, or something that I'm not aware of, help me to be aware of it so I can confess it, too. I thank You that You have forgiven me for the sins I am aware of and I will mention them specifically." We do this because we want our relationship to be right with God. The psalmist reminds us that "if [we] regard wickedness in [our] hearts, the LORD will not hear" our prayers (Psalm 66:18).

The Holy Place

After washing at the laver, you would go into the Holy Place. Entering the Holy Place, you would pass between five large pillars covered with gold, then through a magnificent embroidered curtain of many colors. The first thing we see inside is a candlestick *lampstand* on the left side. The lampstand was large, with seven prongs, and it was the main source of light for the Holy Place. Its light reflecting off of the gold covered walls must have been magnificent. A golden glow filled the room.

This lampstand represents the Holy Spirit to Christians, because it is the Holy Spirit's work to enlighten us. This is based on what was used to make the lampstand shine—the oil. The priests used a special oil in the lampstand. Oil is almost always representative of the Holy Spirit in the Scriptures. In Revelation 5 the Holy Spirit is called the "seven-fold spirit," like the

Lampstand

seven prongs of the lampstand. Seven was the number of "perfection." It was used to refer to deity and completion.

What is important about the Holy Spirit in worship during our time with God? Remember that Jesus said, "When He, the Spirit of truth, comes, He will guide you into all the truth" (John 16:13). It is the Holy Spirit's work to enlighten, to give understanding, and to teach.

Ephesians 5:18 commands us to be filled with the Holy Spirit. I often pray, "Lord, thank You for Your Holy Spirit. Turn the light on and teach me. I'm dependent upon Your Spirit to understand Your truth."

Paul tells us that, if we walk in the Spirit, we will not carry out the desires of the flesh. The desires of the flesh war against the desires of the Spirit. If being full of God's Spirit can help us with our inner desires, then we want to be filled with His Spirit.

The next object that would get your attention as you moved through the Holy Place would be a small gold covered table called the *table of shewbread*. It was about two feet high with a beautiful carved border around its edges. It held specially prepared bread. The use of bread as a biblical symbol is tremendous. The priests place fresh bread weekly on the table of shewbread. It was food for the priests, but was first laid before God. The word shewbread meant "the table of God's presence," or literally, "before my face." It was symbolic of God's provision for their needs—that God is always present to provide for us. As we think about this, we would be reminded to say, "Lord, thank You that You have provided for my needs this day. I don't know how, but I know You will." Philippians 4:13 says, "I can do all things through Christ who strengthens me" (NKJV). Jesus called Himself the Bread of Life and God gives us strength and provides for our needs each day through Christ. We can give thanks for that.

Table of Shewbread

The last piece of furniture in the Holy Place is the *altar of incense*. It was a smaller altar more vertical than the altar of sacrifice. This was the place for intercession. The priest would take coals from the altar of sacrifice, put them on the altar of incense, pour incense on top of those burning coals, and a cloud of sweet-smelling aroma would come up before the veil between the Holy Place and the Holy of Holies. God told the priests it was a sweet-smelling aroma to Him when they interceded for the nation of Israel (Psalm 141:2). Here we are reminded to pray for others. We can pray for our friends, family, and other special needs we know about (Ephesians 6:18).

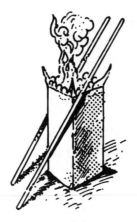

Altar of Incense

No Selfishness

So far, we have not prayed for ourselves. This is by design. By this time we have seen the progressive nature of the Israelites' worship and our own New Testament application; we cannot be accused of simply coming to God to selfishly meet our own needs. We have set our attitude right by offering praise and thanksgiving, sought forgiveness for sins, declared our dependence upon the Spirit, called upon God for strength, and prayed for others. This fulfills our purpose of making our time with God for Him first, then seeking His will for ourselves.

God Opens the Door

The final part of the tabernacle is the Holy of Holies. When Jesus Christ died on the cross, the Bible says that the veil of the temple was torn in two from the top to the bottom. It was a thick veil, two inches thick, running to the top of the temple. No man could have torn it. It was as if God took that veil, ripped it apart, and invited us to come in and be His friends. There were no more barriers. Therefore, we can come into the very presence of God. This area had always been closed to the average Israelite. Only the high priest could go in once each year.

It is in this place that we come before God and share our secret desires, our innermost feelings, our struggles, our fears, the things that bother us, the things with which we need help, and that which we really desire. No matter how large or how small the issue, God is concerned. He is concerned about pain, pleasure, doubt, business—everything! no matter how trivial or selfish it may seem.

It was in the Holy of Holies, at the *mercy seat*, where God allowed His presence to be seen as a cloud. God said to Moses, "And there [at the mercy seat] I will meet with you, and from above the mercy seat . . . I will speak to you about all I will give you . . . " (Exodus 25:22). He was very real to His children. The mercy seat is the reminder that I can come to God for anything, because I'm given mercy and cleansing. It is where I can be honest with God with no fear of rejection.

When the Answer Is No

Charles Spurgeon once told a story about Lady Bolingbroke. During the late sixteenth century she was known as a great woman of prayer. She was once asked by the Lord of Dartmore, "What do you do when you pray and your prayers aren't answered?" She said, "I treat that just like I would a request that I would take before the King of England. I always say, 'Sir, there is something from your greatness that I desire, but if in any way this would detract from your glory and your honor, then I don't want you to answer the request.'" That is the attitude we need as well.

We come before God and say, "God, this is something I want

Mercy Seat

to do or this is something I deeply desire." God can give us those wants, and many times He does. However, sometimes He says, "No, that will not add to My glory and will not really add to your glory like you think it will. I know what is best." We have to accept that a no is as much a part of God's grace as a yes.

A Brief Inspection

I use the plan of the tabernacle as a guide to personal worship and prayer life. It begins with thanksgiving and praise—expressed as I enter through the gate and into the courtyard. This sets my mood to worship God.

The first thing I see is the altar of sacrifice. The altar causes me to realize that I can move no further toward God until I acknowledge that Jesus Christ is the sacrifice for my sins. Until I have trusted Jesus and Him alone for forgiveness by God the Father, I am unable to have a close relationship with God. At this point I say, "Lord, thank You for being my sacrifice. Today I give You my mouth, my lips, my eyes, my ears, my mind, my hands, my feet. . . . Use them for Your glory and Your honor."

Next, I come to the laver, and say, "Lord, point out each sin that I haven't confessed." And I pause and confess what comes to my mind.

From the outer court, I imagine myself going into the Holy Place. It is dark, and the first thing I see is the lampstand. It reminds me to pray about the Spirit. "Fill me, Father, with Your Spirit and control me with Your Spirit. Help me understand Your truth, and teach me by Your Spirit this day."

I would notice the table of shewbread—a reminder of God's provision. "Thank You, Lord, for Your provision for my needs and Your strengthening me for this day."

Then I come before the altar of incense and offer up prayer for others—the ones I love, my friends, and anyone I feel impressed to pray for. Some days I pray only for my family, another day I pray for friends, another day for missionaries, and so on. Too long of a list on any one day can become monotonous, unless you have the time and the desire.

Last of all I come into the Holy of Holies, to the mercy seat, to talk about those deep needs that I have, to express my love to Him, and express whatever is on my heart.

Walk Through the Tabernacle

Outside
- Gates—Thanksgiving
- Courtyard—Praise
- Altar of Sacrifice—Sacrifice for my sin, sacrifice of my life
- Laver—Confession and cleansing

Inside
- Lampstand—Ask Holy Spirit's filling and enlightenment
- Table of Shewbread—God's provision
- Altar of Incense—Prayer for others
- Holy of Holies—Prayer for my needs

Remember these guidelines as you consider the tabernacle as a part of your personal worship:

1. Use it as desired—not as "a must" ritual. Most days I use it—some days I don't. It's an organizer for my prayer life with an easy-to-remember mental picture.
2. Length of time is not important—enjoying it gives it quality. I may spend ten minutes or one hour.
3. Never hold back a pressing prayer need or strong desire just to keep the order. Making a pressing need conform to a sequence is not realistic. We don't do that in any other relationship. God wants you to be yourself when you meet with Him.
4. Don't think of this as a method—but preparation of the heart.

Try this guide in your own prayer life. Whenever you meet with God, see if this doesn't help you enjoy it more.

——— *Reflection* ——————————————————————————

1. Why does God want us to praise Him?
2. Take the model of the tabernacle and rewrite it in your own words. Then try to use it daily for two weeks.

CHAPTER SIXTEEN

Answers to Questions

USE THIS TABLE TO HELP you locate answers to the questions that most concern you about your time with God. (Chapter numbers are in bold type.)

1. How do I listen to God or know when He is speaking to me? **9**
2. How do I handle the "down" times? **12**
3. How do I discipline myself to be more consistent? **12**
4. How do I make more personal applications? **11** and **13**
5. How do I increase my concentration and not let my mind wander? **12**
6. How do I get beyond the feeling that I "have to" have a quiet time? **11**
7. How do I establish momentum? **3** and **4**
8. How do I handle periods of travel and holidays away from home? **12**
9. How do I combine an intellectual study of the Word with the feelings of joy that should accompany the Christian life? **12**
10. How do I cultivate creativity? **11**
11. How do I keep from getting bored with overworked Bible passages? **10**
12. How much should I read and what is the balance between reading and praying? **11** and **12**

13. How flexible should I be with my schedule? **11** and **12**
14. What kind of systematic method would help my quiet time more? **12**
15. What if I miss having my quiet time? How do I handle my guilt? **11** and **12**
16. What do I do when I do not have enough time? **11** and **12**
17. What is "quality" time? **12**
18. How important are emotions and feelings in my devotional life? **3** and **12**
19. When I lose my love for the Lord, how do I make myself love Him again? Or how do I worship when I don't feel like it? **3** and **12**
20. Doesn't God tire of seeing me struggle with the same problems over and over again? **3** and **12**

Bibliography

Devotional Philosophy

Allender, Dan B., Jr., and Tremper Longman, III. *The Cry of the Soul*. Colorado Springs: NavPress, 1994.

Bridges, Jerry. *The Discipline of Grace–God's Role and Our Role in the Pursuit of Holiness*. Colorado Springs: NavPress, 1994.

Colson, Charles. *Loving God*. Grand Rapids: Zondervan, 1983.

Edgar, William. *In Spirit and in Truth*. Downers Grove, Ill.: InterVarsity Press, 1976.

Huggett, Joyce. *The Joy of Listening to God*. Downers Grove, Ill.: InterVarsity Press, 1986.

Lawrence, Brother. *The Practice of the Presence of God*. Old Tappan, N.J.: Revell, 1958.

Longman, Tremper, III. *Reading the Bible with Heart and Soul*. Colorado Springs: NavPress, 1997.

MacArthur, John, Jr. *The Ultimate Priority*. Chicago: Moody Press, 1983.

McGee, J. Vernon. *What Is Worship?* Pasadena, Calif.: Thru the Bible Books, 1972.

Munger, Robert. *My Heart Christ's Home*. Downers Grove, Ill.: InterVarsity Press, 1986.

NavPress. *Appointment with God*. Colorado Springs: NavPress, 1973.

Packer, J. I. *Knowing God*. Downers Grove, Ill.: InterVarsity Press, 1973.

Peterson, Eugene. *Working the Angles: The Shape of Pastoral Integrity*. Grand Rapids: Eerdmans, 1987.

Piper, John. *Desiring God*. Portland, Ore.: Multnomah Press, 1986.

———. *The Pleasures of God*. Portland, Ore.: Multnomah Press, 1991.

Tozer, A. W. *The Pursuit of God*. Camp Hill, Pa.: Christian Publications, Inc., 1982.

———. *Worship, The Missing Jewel of the Evangelical Church*. Camp Hill, Pa.: Christian Publications, Inc., 1996.

Yancey, Philip. *The Jesus I Never Knew*. Grand Rapids: Zondervan, 1995.

Devotional Particulars

Prayer

Bennett, Arthur, ed. *The Valley of Vision–A Collection of Puritan Prayers and Devotions*. Carlisle, Pa.: Banner of Truth, 1975.

Biehl, Bob, and James W. Angelganz. *Praying, How to Start and Keep Going*. Glendale, Calif.: Gospel Light, 1976.

Bounds, E. M. *Power Through Prayer*. Chicago: Moody Press, 1983.

Brandt, Leslie. *Psalms of Praise*. St. Louis: Concordia, 1977.

Campus Crusade for Christ. *The Great Commission Prayer Crusade* Monthly Emphasis Sheet. San Bernardino, Calif.: Campus Crusade for Christ, n.d.

Hallesby, O. *Prayer*. Updated ed. Minneapolis: Augsburg, 1994.

Murray, Andrew. *The Ministry of Intercession*. Chicago: Moody Press, 1982.

———. *The Prayer Life*. Chicago: Moody Press, n.d.

———. *Waiting on God*. Springdale, Pa.: Whitaker House, 1981.

Nicholson, Emily. *Prayer, Talking with God*. Wheaton, Ill.: Scripture Press, 1977.

Peterson, Eugene. *Answering God–The Psalms as Tools for Prayer.* San Francisco: Harper, 1989.

Pollock, Constance and Daniel Pollock, eds. *The Book of Uncommon Prayer.* Nashville: Word, 1996.

Rinker, Rosalind. *Prayer, Conversing with God.* Grand Rapids: Zondervan, 1959.

Sanders, J. Oswald. *Effective Prayer.* Chicago: Moody Press, 1969.

Strauss, Lehman. *Sense and Nonsense About Prayer.* Chicago: Moody Press, 1976.

Unknown Christian. *The Kneeling Christian.* Grand Rapids: Zondervan, 1971.

World Literature Crusade. *Half the World . . . Updated.* Studio City, Calif.: World Literature Crusade, 1974.

Young, David L. *The Life of Prayer.* Austin, Tex.: Scriptural Prayer Emphasis Ministries, International, n.d.

Bible Study

Baughman, Ray E. *Creative Bible Study Methods.* Chicago: Moody Press, 1976.

Bence, Evelyn. *Spiritual Moments with the Great Hymns.* Grand Rapids: Zondervan, 1997.

Calvin, John. *Heart Aflame: Daily Readings from Calvin on the Psalms.* Phillipsburg, N.J.: P&R Publishing, 1999.

Downey, Roy. *Meditation.* Colorado Springs: NavPress, 1976.

Gariepy, Henry. *100 Portraits of Christ.* Wheaton, Ill.: Victor Books, 1987.

Jensen, Irving. *Independent Bible Study.* Chicago: Moody Press, 1963. (Also see Jensen's *Self-study Guide on Topics* and *Every Book of the Bible.*)

LaHaye, Tim. *How to Study the Bible for Yourself.* Rev. and exp. Eugene, Ore.: Harvest House, 1976.

Mickelsen, A. B., and Alvera Mickelsen. *Better Bible Study.* Glendale, Calif.: Gospel Light, 1977.

NavPress. *A Primer for Meditation.* Colorado Springs: NavPress, n.d.

———. *Studies in Christian Living.* Colorado Springs: NavPress, 1965.

NavPress Staff. *The Topical Memory System.* Colorado Springs: NavPress, 1969.

Packer, J. I. *The Apostles Creed.* Wheaton, Ill.: Tyndale House, 1983.

Peterson, Janice Stubbs, ed. *Living the Message: Daily Readings With Eugene Peterson.* San Francisco: Harper, 1996.

Ray, David. *The Art of Christian Meditation.* Wheaton, Ill.: Tyndale House, 1977.

Sanchez, George. *Changing Your Thought Patterns.* Colorado Springs: NavPress, n.d.

Sproul, R. C. *Knowing Scripture.* Downers Grove, Ill.: InterVarsity Press, 1978.

Wald, Oletta. *The Joy of Discovery.* Minneapolis: Augsburg, 1956.

Walk Thru the Bible Ministries. *The Daily Walk.* Mt. Morris, Ill.: Walk Thru the Bible Ministries, n.d.

Devotional Practice

Hughes, Milt. *Spiritual Journey Notebook.* Nashville, Tenn.: The Sunday School Board of the Southern Baptist Convention, 1974.

Lord, Peter M. *The 2959 Plan.* Titusville, Fla.: Agape Ministries, 1976.

HAVE YOUR HEARD OF

The Four Spiritual Laws?

Just as there are physical laws that govern the physical universe, so are there spiritual laws which govern your relationship with God.

1 LAW ONE

GOD **LOVES** YOU, AND OFFERS A WONDERFUL **PLAN** FOR YOUR LIFE.

God's Love
"For God so loved the world, that He gave His only begotten Son, that whoever believes in Him should not perish, but have eternal life" (John 3:16).

God's Plan
(Christ speaking) "I came that they might have life, and might have it abundantly" (that it might be full and meaningful) (John 10:10).

Why is it that most people are not experiencing the abundant life? Because . . .

2 LAW TWO

MAN IS **SINFUL** AND **SEPARATED** FROM GOD. THEREFORE, HE CANNOT KNOW AND EXPERIENCE GOD'S LOVE AND PLAN FOR HIS LIFE.

Used by permission of Thomas Nelson Publishers, Inc.

Man Is Sinful

"For all have sinned and fall short of the glory of God" (Romans 3:23).

Man Is Separated

"For the wages of sin is death" (spiritual separation from God) (Romans 6:23).

The third law explains the only way to bridge this gulf . . .

3 LAW THREE

JESUS CHRIST IS GOD'S **ONLY** PROVISION FOR MAN'S SIN. THROUGH HIM YOU CAN KNOW AND EXPERIENCE GOD'S LOVE AND PLAN FOR YOUR LIFE.

He Died in Our Place

"But God demonstrates His own love toward us, in that while we were yet sinners, Christ died for us" (Romans 5:8).

He Rose from the Dead

"Christ died for our sins . . . He was buried . . . He was raised on the third day, according to the Scriptures . . . He appeared to Peter, then to the twelve. After that He appeared to more than five hundred . . ." (1 Corinthians 15:3–6).

He Is the Only Way to God

"Jesus said to him, 'I am the way, and the truth, and the life; no one comes to the Father, but through Me' " (John 14:6).

It is not enough just to know these three laws.

4 LAW FOUR

WE MUST INDIVIDUALLY **RECEIVE** JESUS CHRIST AS SAVIOR AND LORD; THEN WE CAN KNOW AND EXPERIENCE GOD'S LOVE AND PLAN FOR OUR LIVES.

We Must Receive Christ

"But as many as received Him, to them He gave the right to become children of God, even to those who believe in His name" (John 1:12).

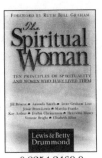

We Receive Christ Through Faith

"For by grace you have been saved through faith; and that not of your-selves, it is the gift of God; not as a result of works, that no one should boast" (Ephesians 2:8,9).

When We Receive Christ, We Experience a New Birth.
(Read John 3:1–8).

YOU CAN RECEIVE CHRIST RIGHT NOW BY FAITH THROUGH PRAYER.

(Prayer is talking with God)

God knows your heart and is not so concerned with your words as He is with the attitude of your heart. The following is a suggested prayer:

> *"Lord Jesus, I need You. Thank You for dying on the cross for my sins. I open the door of my life and receive You as my Savior and Lord. Thank You for forgiving my sins and giv-ing me eternal life. Take control of the throne of my life. Make me the kind of person You want me to be."*

Does this prayer express the desire of your heart?

If it does, pray this prayer right now, and Christ will come into your life, as He promised.